# THE

# GUESTS

***THEY WEREN'T INVITED***

***AND NOW THEY'RE GOING TO PAY***

**FOR VERNLEIGH:**

**YOUR COVER PHOTOGRAPH INSPIRED ME**

**TO KILL PEOPLE IN WAYS I NEVER**

**WOULD HAVE DREAMED OF BEFORE.**

## PROLOGUE

Rebecca Green's mother always maintained there was good in everyone. Agnes Green was born four years before the start of the Second World War and when she returned to London after the evacuation, she'd experienced things no ten-year-old should ever have to go through. Hardship had made her see the world differently and as the post-war austerity faded and the world began to heal from the wounds of the war, the fifties was a time of hope and promise. Agnes looked to the future with optimism – she was able to look past the murky surface and find goodness in everyone she met.

Rebecca came into the world at the end of the 1950s – she was born into a time of change, and she too found the hidden depths many others couldn't see. The angry lollipop lady outside the school Rebecca's grandchildren attended was a good example. Psycho Sue was a fierce, hefty woman who instilled the fear of God in everyone, young and old, but Rebecca was able to look past the terrifying exterior and see something different in Psycho Sue. Here was a woman who had suffered terrible pain in her life and her gruff persona was simply a result of that suffering. It didn't take long for Rebecca and Psycho Sue to become friends.

No, Rebecca Green could always find goodness inside a person eventually.

Until now.

The thugs and hooligans enjoying a stag party at the HomeFromHome weekend rental next door were an exception to this rule. They'd announced their arrival at lunchtime with a car sound system that had shaken the foundations of Rebecca and Henry Green's cottage – it was now almost ten at night and the noise had increased to such a level Henry could no longer hear the television.

This couldn't go on - Rebecca had told Henry. This had to stop. Henry had always done his best to avoid confrontation and he'd argued they were only letting their hair down – blowing off a bit of steam. The *guests* were only a nuisance at weekends, he'd said.

But Rebecca wasn't going to put up with it anymore. And as the she gazed out onto the back garden and felt the vibration of the bass speakers on the window, an idea started to take shape in her head. It was late May and the garden was in full bloom. The belladonna Rebecca had recently acquired had taken well to its new home and the pinkish-purple of the foxgloves had almost reached the top of the fence. It had been a close call the first time the police had come calling, but this time Rebecca decided they wouldn't have a clue what was happening. They wouldn't know where to start looking.

A booming voice from next door announced another round of drinking games was in order and at the same time an empty beer bottle was flung over the fence into Rebecca's prized rose bushes.

There was no good in these people, she decided. No good whatsoever. And it was high time someone put an end to the hell these HomeFromHome rentals were causing for the residents nearby.

## CHAPTER ONE

*Six weeks earlier*

"It looks perfect," Rebecca Green swung the laptop around so her husband Henry could get a better look.

Henry put down his newspaper and glanced at the screen. "It's lovely."

"The village is called Frisk," Rebecca told him. "It's about five miles east of Milford on Sea right at the tip of the New Forest National Park."

"Didn't we go there once when Colin and Phoebe were small?"

"That was Highcliffe," Rebecca said. "But it's not far from there. The cottage has a view right across to the Isle of Wight."

"Lovely," Henry said once more.

"We can afford it," Rebecca continued. "The estate agent said we'll sell this place in a flash – let's go and have a look at the cottage."

"It's supposed to rain later," Henry said. "It's a long way to drive in the rain."

"I don't mean right now. We'll have to make an appointment. We can kill two birds with one stone. The estate agent reckons there's a waiting list for houses in this area and we'll sell quickly. We'll put our house on the market right away. The cottage is going for a bargain. Property in that part of the country usually sells for almost twice what they're asking for it."

Henry looked more carefully at the screen. "Why's it so cheap? What's wrong with it? There has to be a catch."

"They probably want a quick sale, and that's why we need to act fast. Someone else will snap it up if we don't. I'm going to make that appointment."

Rebecca had retired from her job at Higgins IT the previous year and after forty years teaching English Henry had stopped working soon afterwards. All their lives they'd dreamed of a house by the sea and the cottage in the small village of Frisk was an opportunity too good to pass up.

"What about Colin and Phoebe?" Henry said. "What about the grandkids? Who's going to help out when they need someone to walk them to school?"

"Colin is forty-two, love," Rebecca reminded him. "And Phoebe is almost forty – I think they're old enough to look after themselves. And the twins will be old enough to walk to school on their own next term."

"We'll never see them," Henry hadn't quite finished. "If we move to Frisk, we'll never see the grandkids. And what if Phoebe falls off the wagon again and goes back to her old ways? Who's going to be there to pick up the pieces?"

A few years ago, Phoebe had got in with the wrong crowd – she'd just come out of a long-term relationship and what this crowd offered seemed attractive at the time. After a stint in rehab, she'd managed to sort out her life but Henry and Rebecca knew there was always a chance of relapse.

"We won't be moving to the other side of the world," Rebecca said. "It's an eighty-mile trip down the M3. Phoebe is old enough to look after herself. It's what we've always dreamed about, Henry. A cottage by the sea."

Henry picked the newspaper back up.

"Shall I make that appointment, then?" Rebecca wasn't giving up.

"I suppose it won't do any harm to have a look," Henry said and returned his attention back to his newspaper.

"It'll do us the world of good. We've been in this house far too long."

Rebecca and Henry had bought the three-bedroom semi-detached house in Wimbledon soon after they were married. Rebecca had been pregnant with Colin at the time and, even though the area wasn't particularly upmarket it was all they could afford on Henry's teaching salary. Rebecca had stayed at home and Phoebe came along a couple of years later. When the children were old enough to go to school Rebecca had worked various office jobs.

House prices in Wimbledon had soared in recent years and the estate agent Rebecca had spoken to hadn't been exaggerating when he said there was a waiting list for houses on their estate. Rebecca estimated they would easily be able to afford the cottage in Frisk with plenty of money left over.

Henry put down his paper and eased himself up from the armchair.

"The sea air will do wonders for your arthritis," Rebecca told him. "It's been proven."

"Tea?" Henry asked.

"I could murder one."

"When did you go and see the estate agent?"

"I didn't. It's all online these days – there's no need to go from office to office looking at bad photographs in the front window. I sent an email enquiry and he phoned me back. You need to get more up to date, dear."

"I've never been comfortable with this new technology nonsense. I'll put the kettle on. What time are Colin and Susan coming round?"

"That's tomorrow," Rebecca said.

"Ah, right. The old brain doesn't work as well as it used to, now I'm retired. Do you want honey or sugar?"

"Sugar. Just one spoonful. Just think – in a few months we could be looking out across the Solent at the Isle of Wight."

"I suppose it beats having to look at Mr and Mrs Havisham's beaten-up old camper van. I'll make that tea. I'll drink a cup and take His Lordship there out for a quick walk."

His Lordship was their ten-year-old Jack Russel, Alfred. The dog was in danger of slipping off the sofa. His mouth was wide open and drool was hanging from his lips.

"Alfie is going to love the cottage," Rebecca said. "We can take him for long walks on the beach."

"You'll have to get him off his chair first," Henry looked at the lazy Jack Russell. "I've never met such a slothful dog."

"I spoke to the estate agent," Rebecca said an hour later.

Henry had returned with an exhausted Jack Russell in tow. The dog made a beeline for his favourite chair as soon as he got home.

"He's bringing someone round later to take a few photos of the house," Rebecca continued. "And he's made an appointment for us to see the cottage in Frisk on Monday afternoon."

"Monday?" Henry said.

"Have you got something else to do on Monday?"

"Of course not. I believe my diary is fairly bereft of engagements for the foreseeable future, I just think Monday is a strange day to view a property."

"Mr Needham from Needham's Properties reckons Monday is the only day he can get away from London."

"Doesn't the owner of the cottage work?"

"Apparently not. The owner doesn't live there, anyway, and Mr Needham also mentioned something about getting in quick. According to him, we're not the only ones viewing the cottage on Monday."

"He would say that, wouldn't he?" Henry said. "I don't trust estate agents."

"I told you, the place is going for a song, so we need to get moving on this. We can make a day of it and grab a bite to eat by the sea while we're there. This is going to change our lives, Henry. This is going to be the best decision we've ever made. I suppose I ought to do a bit of a tidy up before Mr Needham gets here."

## CHAPTER TWO

Darren Needham was an extremely tall man but it seemed like a large proportion of that height was neck. He had to stoop to get under the door frame and his giraffe-like neck looked like it might snap at any time. He'd brought a young woman with him and Rebecca assumed she was the photographer.

Henry was engrossed in a book in the living room when they arrived.

"Henry," Rebecca said. "The photographer is here."

Henry stood up with a groan. "I'll make myself scarce, then."

"There's no need for that." It was Darren Needham.

Henry looked up at him and straight away he didn't like what he saw. Henry had never trusted estate agents and he took an instant dislike to Darren Needham.

"Emma will make sure you're not in any of the photos," Darren added.

"Charming," Henry said under his breath.

"Alfie," Rebecca said and gave the dog a gentle nudge off the sofa. "Go and get some fresh air. You're going to get fat."

Darren Needham bent down to stroke the Jack Russell. "I've always had a thing for dogs."

Alfred was suddenly wide awake. He stared at the estate agent's approaching hand and bared his teeth. A low, guttural growl could be heard from somewhere inside the dog's throat.

"Alfred Green," Rebecca said. "That's not nice."

"Good boy," Henry said in a voice no louder than a whisper. "I'll take him outside to the back garden."

"Would you like something to drink?" Rebecca asked Darren Needham.

"No thank you," Darren said. "I've got a busy schedule today."

"I suppose in your line of work weekends are the busiest times."

"They most certainly are. Let's get down to business, shall we? Emma will crack on while we discuss the other matter."

"Other matter?" Henry said.

"Sea View Cottage."

"Sea View Cottage?" Henry repeated and grimaced at his wife. "You didn't tell me we were considering relocating to a cliché."

"Henry," Rebecca said. "That's enough. You'll have to excuse my husband, Mr Needham – Henry still thinks he's an English teacher."

"I was never very good at English," Darren said.

"Hmm," Henry said but the expression on his wife's face warned him it would be wise not to say anything else.

The photographer informed them she was finished in the kitchen, so Rebecca, Henry and Darren sat down at the small table in there. Darren unzipped a bag, took out a laptop and switched it on.

"This thing sometimes takes a while to boot up."

"It's one of my pet hates," Rebecca said. "That's why I get the latest processor every couple of years."

Darren looked surprised. "You know something about computers, then?"

Henry laughed. "What my Rebecca doesn't know about computers isn't worth knowing."

"I worked for a big IT company just off Green Park," Rebecca elaborated. "I retired last year."

"Impressive," Darren said. "Here we go. I don't need to tell you that time is of the essence. Sea View Cottage has only been on the market a couple of days and already we've been inundated with enquiries."

"Why is it so cheap?" Henry asked.

"The owner wants a quick sale."

"That's what I thought," Rebecca said.

"Can I make a suggestion?" Darren said.

"Of course."

"You both seem to have your heads screwed on and I got a good vibe from both of you the moment I walked in. I can see you want the cottage and I want you to have it. Opportunities like these don't come along very often. I know – I've been in this business for quite some time, and I know a bargain when I see one."

"Why don't you buy the place then?" Henry said.

"Henry," Rebecca said. "Don't be rude."

Darren laughed a feeble laugh. "It's alright. I like a sense of humour as much as the next man. Right, what I've done for you is this: like I said we've got a few other people viewing the property on Monday, but I've put you to the top of the list. Is half-one, Monday afternoon fine by you?"

"Perfect," Rebecca said. "We'll be there."

"Do you have any idea what you want for this place?" Darren asked. "A rough idea is fine."

"I had a look on the net," Rebecca said. "And it's hard to gauge as there are very few other properties in this area on the market."

"That's true, and that's why I would very much like this listing. We sold a three-bedroom just off the Southside Common last month for eight-fifty."

"Eight-hundred-and-fifty thousand?" Henry said.

"And that was probably the last bargain to be had in this area. If you want a quick sale, I'd suggest somewhere in the region of nine-hundred."

Rebecca did some quick mental arithmetic. Sea View Cottage was on the market for seven-hundred-and-fifty-thousand pounds – even with the estate agent's commission they would be left with almost a hundred-thousand.

"I didn't realise this place was worth so much," she said.

"That's why it pays to go with an honest estate agent," Darren said. "At Needham Properties we don't go for the quick money – we're invested in the future and that's why *integrity* is our verb of choice. There's a bit of English language for you, Mr Green."

He grinned at Henry.

Henry debated whether to point out *integrity* was actually a noun but decided he couldn't be bothered.

"So," Darren said. "We're decided on nine-hundred, then?"

"I think it's a fair price for a quick sale," Rebecca said. "Wouldn't you agree, Henry?"

"I haven't the foggiest idea," Henry said.

"Nine-hundred it is then," Darren carried on, unperturbed. "Is there anything I need to know about the property before we proceed? Any problems with damp? Leaking roofs and the like? These days we're obliged to outline any defects."

"Nothing," Rebecca said. "The bottom of the shed in the garden is a bit rotten but that's about it."

"I wouldn't worry about a few planks of wood. Anything else?"

"The camper van across the road is a bit of an eyesore," Henry added.

"That's a matter for the council," Darren told him. "We won't mention that. I took the liberty of bringing the contract with me today. If you could just have a read through it and tick the relevant boxes, we'll get the ball rolling."

"You want us to sign something now?" Henry said.

"I'll leave you in peace," Darren said. "If you don't mind, I'll have a wander around and get a feel for the property. It'll give me a better understanding about what I'm going to put on the website."

"I don't trust him," Henry said when he heard the back door close. Darren Needham had gone outside to inspect the back garden. Alfred started to bark and Henry smiled.

"You don't trust anybody," Rebecca said. "Needham's are reputable estate agents. They've been around for donkey's years."

"He's too pushy for my liking. And Alfred doesn't like him – that's enough for me to know he can't be trusted."

"He's trying to do his best for us. He wants us to have Sea View Cottage."

"And I don't like that name. It's something you'd see on the esplanade in a place like Brighton. It's rather platitudinous."

"We can change it. Let's just read through the contract and see what it says."

"What commission is he ripping us off for?" Henry asked.

"Six percent. It's a fair commission. Estate agents don't just find a seller and a buyer and take their commission. There's the advertising costs, legal advice and all that. They take care of the nitty-gritty and make it as painless as possible for all parties."

"Six percent of nine-hundred grand is over fifty-thousand, love. That's a lot of money."

"It's the standard commission. He's coming back in."

"How are we doing?" Darren pointed to the papers on the table.

"We need some time to look over the contract in peace," Henry said.

"Like I said, time is of the essence here. The quicker we sell this house the sooner you can be looking out to sea."

"We won't be rushed into a decision like this."

"I'll scan and email them over to you when we've gone through them," Rebecca suggested. "I've got your email address."

"That can work," Darren said. "And I'll send you a link to the website listing when it's live."

"Great."

Darren looked at his watch. "I'd better be going. I'm showing a property in Stratford in half an hour."

"Good luck with that," Henry said. "The Hammers are playing at home today. Traffic is going to be a nightmare."

"I know a way around. I'll be in touch."

"Nine-hundred-thousand," Rebecca said to Henry when Darren and Emma had left. "Who'd have thought it?"

"I can't even remember what we paid for the house forty-odd years ago," he said.

"Me neither. We can buy Sea View Cottage and still have money left over."

"I'll think about it," Henry conceded. "On one condition."

"We change the name?" Rebecca guessed.

"That's right."

"What did you have in mind?"

"Something will come to me when I see the place."

"We're really going to do this, aren't we?" Rebecca asked.

"I suppose a change is as good as a rest," Henry said. "And speaking of which, I'm going to have an hours' nap – the sound of that estate agent's voice has left me rather weary."

# CHAPTER THREE

The rain clouds that had opened up over the City of London overnight had drifted off to the west. Henry Green opened one eye and was immediately aware of the drone of the vacuum cleaner downstairs. The clock on the bedside table told him it was just after eight in the morning.
*Why the hell is she hoovering up at this time on a Sunday*?

Colin, Susan and the grandkids were coming for lunch but Rebecca had never bothered to clean up before when they were due to come over. The incessant hum of the vacuum cleaner was still reverberating around the house and for some reason it made Henry feel agitated. It was Sunday morning and he believed certain things to be sacred. Hoovering on a Sunday morning was all wrong. The dead weight at the bottom of the bed told Henry he wasn't the only one who found the vacuum cleaner offensive – somehow Alfred had crept inside the room, unseen and was now passed out on Henry's legs. Henry shifted the Jack Russell to the side and got out of bed. He did what he needed to do in the bathroom and went downstairs.

He turned on the kettle and the sound of the vacuum cleaner stopped. The silence that followed didn't last long as Henry heard Rebecca drag the hoover into the dining room and soon it started up again. Henry made himself a cup of tea and rubbed his temples. The constant drone was giving him a headache. Alfred ambled in and headed straight for the back door.
"Good God, woman," Henry said and went outside to the back garden.

The Jack Russel followed him outside. The plastic garden furniture was soaked so Henry tipped up the chairs and put his tea on the table. The rain that had fallen overnight had stained the wooden fence separating their house from next door dark brown in places. Henry sipped his tea and looked at the oak tree at the bottom of the garden. Droplets of water were dripping from its leaves and falling onto the lawn below. Henry remembered planting the tree when he and Rebecca first moved in. That was over forty years ago now and it made him realise they'd been here for two-thirds of their lives. Their children knew no other home while they were growing up and there were more memories embedded in the bricks and mortar here than Henry cared to think about.

"Forty-three-years," Henry said to himself. "Where did the time go?"

He didn't get the chance to dwell on the thought. The back door opened and Rebecca appeared, holding a vacuum cleaner bag in her hand.

"Open the wheelie bin for me, will you?"

Henry lifted the lid. "Why on earth are you up hoovering on a Sunday morning? It's just plain rude."

"I couldn't sleep," Rebecca banged the hoover bag against the inside of the bin. "I checked my emails and found out the listing for our house is live. It's a very good advert and Needham Properties have made the listing a premium one to attract more attention. Anyway, Mr Needham phoned me just after seven to tell me he has someone interested already. A cash buyer."

"What else are they going to pay with?" Henry said. "Bananas?"

"It means we don't have to go through the rigmarole of waiting for a buyer to get a mortgage arranged. Mr Needham told me we could be in the cottage before the end of next month."

"Surely that's a bit optimistic?"

"Not according to Mr Needham. He's bringing the interested buyer for a viewing at lunchtime. That's why I was tidying up a bit."

"But Colin and Susan and the grandkids are coming over," Henry reminded her.

"Mr Needham said it's fine. He's positive the client is just going through the motions. He made up his mind as soon as he saw the ad on the website. I've got a good feeling about this, Henry. This is going to be a remarkable new beginning for us both."

"I suppose I ought to clear away the clutter in my study then. Make the place a bit more presentable."

Rebecca linked her arm with his. "We're going to live out the rest of our lives with peace and quiet and a sea breeze. This is what we've been dreaming about for all these years."

* * *

Colin and Susan Green arrived just before noon. Katie and Paul nodded their greetings and headed upstairs to the spare bedroom. The nine-year-old twins always spent most of their time playing games on the PC on the desk in there.

"Not so fast you two," Rebecca stopped them halfway up. "We've got someone coming to look at the house in a bit, and I don't want you making a mess up there."

"We won't," the twins said in unison.

Colin's eyes narrowed. "You didn't tell us you had the place on the market."

"We didn't know ourselves until yesterday, son," Henry said. "Your mother found a cottage going for a song and everything happened so fast."

"It's beautiful," Rebecca said. "It's in this little village down by Milford on Sea – it looks out onto the Isle of Wight and it's priced to sell."

"How much?"

Colin was a Chartered Accountant and he was not shy talking about the price of things.

"Seven-fifty," Henry told him.

"What's wrong with it?" Susan asked.

"That's what I said," Henry told her.

"The owner just wants a quick sale," Rebecca insisted. "That's the only reason it's going so cheap."

"You don't get a place down there with a sea view for that price," Colin said. "Unless there's a catch."

"There's no catch. The owner wants shut and we're going to go for it."

"It sounds dodgy to me," Colin wasn't giving up.

"The estate agent is coming round later to show a prospective buyer the house so you can speak to him about it if you like."

"I'll do that. You have to be so careful these days. It's probably all run-down and in need of a load of money spent on it."

"Not according to the photos," Rebecca said. "Anyway, your dad and me are going down to have a look tomorrow so we'll see if it needs any work done on it then."

"Do you want a beer, son?" Henry changed the subject.

Colin looked to Susan for approval.

"I don't mind driving later," she said.

"Thanks, love," Colin said. "It's been a nightmare of a week. We almost lost the Burton account and old Fuller was like a bear with a sore head."

"Why don't you start up on your own?" Rebecca said. "Surely, you've got enough of a client base now to poach a few of them away from Fuller."

"It'll mean more money," Henry said.

"And more stress," Susan said. "No thank you very much. At least at Fuller Colin can come home on a Friday and leave work behind."

"Working for Fuller isn't too bad," Colin said. "Most of the time."

"Shall we sit in the dining room?" Rebecca suggested. "Tables laid. The roast still has another hour or so to go."

"Can I see the cottage?" Susan asked.

Rebecca fetched her laptop from the sideboard and switched it on. She'd bookmarked the link and brought it up in seconds.

Susan looked at the main photograph on the listing. "That is gorgeous. And is that the view?"

"Stunning, isn't it?" Rebecca said.

"Let's have a look," Colin said.

He got up from his chair and stood behind his wife.

"The cottage is situated in an elevated part of the quaint village of Frisk," he read the description. "Which affords it unobstructed views over the Solent and the Isle of Wight. The east-facing position ensures hours of sunshine all year round."

"You'll be able to watch the sunrise over the island," Susan said.

"Situated in a row of similar properties," Colin carried on reading. "Sea View Cottage offers the best of both worlds."

"We're changing the name if we do buy it," Henry said.

"With its unbeatable views from the two east-facing bedrooms and the tranquil terraced garden," Colin read. "This is a home for those wishing to live life at a slower pace."

"I don't know who comes up with this drivel," Henry said. "Why can't they just say it's a three-bedroom cottage with a view of the sea? End of story. And the grammar is terrible. What's happened to the good-old semi-colon these days?"

"I think it sounds like a dream home," Susan said.

"And it's got three bedrooms," Rebecca said. "So, when you come and stay with the grandkids there'll be plenty of room for you."

"It really is a dream home," Susan said.

## CHAPTER FOUR

"It's a dream home," Darren Needham said.

"Sorry about the mess," Rebecca said to the man and woman the estate agent had brought round. "We've not long finished eating. We've got our son, his wife and the grandkids here."

Alfred had taken a shine to the woman. The Jack Russell sat at her feet and looked up at her with love in his eyes.

"It feels lived-in," the woman said. "And this little dog is adorable."

She patted him on the head and he rolled over onto his back.

"Sorry about Alfie," Rebecca said. "He seems to have taken a liking to you."

"I love dogs," she said and looked at the man she was with. "We should get a dog when we move in. There's plenty of places to walk a dog around here."

"I'll give it some thought," the man said and cast a disapproving glance at Alfred.

The woman was now rubbing his belly.

Rebecca guessed her age to be around mid-twenties. The man she was with looked quite a bit older than her. Darren had introduced them as Bonnie and Vincent Lawton. Henry and Colin had been told to hide out in the garden with a few cans of beer. Katie and Paul had made a beeline for the computer in the spare room as soon as they'd finished eating.

"It's in a well sought-after area," Darren continued. "You've got the parks and of course Wimbledon village. All within walking distance from here."

"What about schools?" Bonnie asked.

"Do you have children?" Susan said.

"Not yet, but one has to plan ahead, doesn't one?"

Rebecca got the impression this wasn't how this young woman had always spoken. The East End twang was almost impossible to disguise.

"Well," Darren said. "There's the High School by the Centre Court Shopping Centre, and King's College of course."

"Of course," Bonnie said.

"And there's a few very good primary schools in the area," Rebecca said.

Bonnie looked up at her husband. "I love it, darling."

"It does appear to tick all the boxes," Vincent agreed. "And I imagine the price is negotiable?"

"I'd have to discuss that in private with Mr and Mrs Green," Darren said. "But I have to be honest with you - the property was only listed yesterday and already I've had over two-dozen enquiries."

Vincent Lawton nodded. "Alright. What do you need me to sign? To secure the deal, I mean?"

"If you can just complete an offer to purchase, we'll finalise everything in the morning."

This came as quite a shock to Rebecca. Everything was happening so quickly and reality was sinking in.

"We've had many happy memories here," she said to Vincent. "I'm sure you and your wife will have many more."

Vincent Lawton nodded again. "Very good. We have to be off – my lawyers will be in touch with Needham Properties first thing tomorrow."

"As easy as that?" Rebecca said.

She'd just watched as Vincent and Bonnie Lawton had driven off in a black Porsche 4x4.

"I'm going to be brutally honest with you, Mrs Green," Darren said.

The way he lowered his giraffe-like neck when he said this made him resemble a naughty schoolboy.

"I shouldn't really be disclosing well-guarded estate agent secrets, but I really like you and Mr Green. You're good people. I had Mr and Mrs Lawton in mind the moment I found out you intended to sell. An estate agent doesn't simply put a house on the market and wait for it to sell – a good estate agent understands the needs of the client, and that's why I knew Mr and Mrs Lawton would jump at the chance to buy this exceptional property. Where is Mr Green? I'd like to discuss Sea View Cottage with you both."

"I'll go and get him," Susan offered.

She returned a short while later with Henry and Colin. Both of them reeked of beer.

"This is my son, Colin," Rebecca told Darren.

Colin was a short man and he had to crane his neck to look up at the gangly estate agent's face.

Darren held out his hand. "Nice to meet you. I'm sure your mother would like to be the one to pass on the good news."

Colin shook the hand. "Good news?"

"They want to buy the house," Rebecca told Henry and Colin.

"Just like that?" Colin said.

"I knew they wanted it," Darren said. "That's why I brought them here first. Now, it's a cash deal and as such everything is going to move along much faster than if we had to wait for mortgage advisers and surveyors and the like. My team will expedite the process further and I'd say the whole transaction could be completed in as little as two weeks."

"Two weeks?" Henry said.

"Give or take. And that means Sea View Cottage is as good as yours. If you still want the property, that is."

"We do," Rebecca said. "We do, don't we, Henry?"

"Slow down." It was Colin. "This is all happening far too quickly for my liking. You don't just fork out that kind of money at the drop of a hat. You need to make absolutely certain everything is in order."

"I assure you, it is, Mr Green," Darren said.

"Give us a few days," Colin suggested. "I want to do some homework on this Sea View Cottage before my mother and father make such a drastic decision."
"That's entirely up to you," Darren said. "I can understand your misgivings, but you have to see it from my perspective. I have an obligation to my clients - buyers and sellers alike, and I owe it to them to act in their best interests. I've already informed your parents of the probable outcome if they were to delay any further."
"We could lose the cottage, Col," Rebecca said.
"And another opportunity like this might not arise for a very long time, if ever. The owner of Sea View Cottage is not an unreasonable woman but I believe I would be derelict in my duty if I delayed the possible sale of the property. I have other buyers lined up. Some of them are cash buyers."

"I need another beer," Colin said. "Can I get you one?"
Darren paused for a moment. "I think a beer would go down very well, thank you."
"I'll get them," Henry offered.
"I'm not saying this is some kind of scam," Colin said. "Isn't there another way to make sure my parents don't lose the cottage while giving them some more time?"

Henry came in with three glasses of beer. He handed one to his son and one to Darren Needham.
Darren took a long sip. "Cheers. There might be a way around this."
"A way around what?" Henry said.
"Doing anything too hasty," Colin told him.
"Come and have a look at the cottage tomorrow like we arranged," Darren nodded down to Colin. "You're welcome to come too if it will help put your mind at rest. Then, if you decide it's what you're looking for we can work on a time-bound contract."

"I'm not following you," Henry said.

"You'd sign a contract that is only valid for a certain amount of time," Colin said.

"That's right," Darren finished what was left in his glass. "It will probably take at least two weeks for the deal on this place to go through, so we'll make that the benchmark."

"What if it takes longer for the money to come through for this house?" Susan joined in.

"That's the beauty of that kind of contract. There's nothing in the law that prevents me from drawing up an offer to purchase and another contract with another potential buyer in the meantime, taking your offer into account. In essence you'll have plenty of time to make up your mind for certain if Sea View Cottage is for you."

Colin frowned. He left the room and returned with more drinks.

"Make it three weeks and you've got a deal."

"I'm not sure I can do that," Darren said as he poured the beer into his glass.

"Think of it as insurance for everyone," Colin explained. "If the deal with the Lawton's takes longer than two weeks for some unforeseen reason at least then my parents won't lose out on the cottage because they ran out of time according to the contract."

Darren Needham appeared to be mulling this over. He swigged his beer, lowered the glass then took another, much larger drink.

"OK," he said. "We've got a deal."

Colin grinned and shook Darren's hand. He felt much more comfortable about his parents' rather rash decision to sell their house and move to Sea View Cottage.

"I'd better get off," Darren said. "This beer has gone straight to my head. I very rarely drink you see and I hope the alcohol hasn't made me agree to something I might come to regret. I'll have the seller send over a signed contract agreeing to the terms we've spoken of and I'll bring it with me to the cottage tomorrow."

"That's put my mind at rest," Colin said to his parents when Darren Needham had left. "And I actually feel quite smug. It's not every day you get the chance to out-bullshit an estate agent. You get the opportunity to think carefully about what you're buying and if it's not the right move you can change your minds and back out."

"I'm glad you were here," Rebecca said. "All that legal stuff was baffling."

"I had absolutely no idea what he was babbling on about," Henry said. "Was he even speaking English?"

"It's all quite straightforward when you start to understand it." Colin said.

What Colin *didn't* understand was he'd all but sealed his parents' fate. Once the contract was signed Rebecca and Henry Green would be bound by it no matter what. Colin had fallen for the oldest estate agent trick in the book - make the client believe a deal is strictly on their terms and they won't pay too much attention to the details. Throw a *dream* property into the mix and the deal is as good as in the bag.

## CHAPTER FIVE

The south London sky was grey and dreary as Rebecca and Henry set off but neither of them paid much attention to it. This was the start of a new beginning – a new chapter in their lives and the grim weather in Wimbledon was the furthest thing from their minds. And when they picked up the M3 at Sunbury and saw the clear skies further south Rebecca saw it as a sign – a good omen. They were heading in the right direction. Their dream of a cottage by the sea was about to become a reality. They'd debated whether to take the dog with them but decided against it. Alfred could be a bit of a handful when they took him anywhere in the car and Rebecca wanted to inspect their future new home in peace. They'd left the Jack Russell asleep upstairs in the spare room and knew he probably wouldn't stir until they arrived back.

"Do you see that?" Rebecca pointed out of the window at the grim weather behind them and the sunshine up ahead. "That's us. That's where we're heading and that's what we're leaving behind. We should have left London years ago."

"I'm actually quite scared," Henry admitted. "This is a big step to make at our age."

"Lots of people do it. Lots of people do what we're doing."

"Not in Wimbledon they don't. I don't know anybody who has, anyway."

"They just don't have our sense of adventure."

"You don't think we're too old?"

"Nonsense. Sixty is the new forty. We've got years of sun and sea air ahead of us."

They drove in silence for the next ten miles. Henry kept his speed to a steady fifty-miles-per-hour. They passed under the M25 and a sign on the side of the road told him Farnborough was about thirty miles away.

"That's London behind us, then," he said. "I had a look at the map last night and we continue on the M3 until we reach Eastleigh. Then we bypass Southampton on the M27 and take a left onto a B road. I thought it would be nice to drive through the New Forest."

"It sounds lovely," Rebecca agreed.

"We'll head as far south as Lymington and it shouldn't be too far from there. If we get lost, we can always ask for directions."

"I'll put the GPS on."

"I didn't know we had one."

"I've got one on my phone," Rebecca told him. "Most phones have them these days."

"We're going to be early," Rebecca said as they passed the outskirts of Basingstoke. "It's still only half-nine. I don't know why we set off so early."

"I wasn't sure how the traffic would be," Henry said. "Or the weather. You know I don't like driving fast in bad weather."

"It doesn't matter. We can take a slow drive through the New Forest – we can take it all in. We're going to have all of that on our doorstep soon."

They were almost at Winchester when Rebecca's mobile phone started to ring. She took it out of her handbag and answered it.

"Mrs Green." It was Darren Needham. "I'm sorry to do this but something has come up and I won't be able to make it to Frisk today."

"But we're over halfway there," Rebecca told him.

"I'm not cancelling the viewing, Mrs Green, I just wanted to let you know another agent will be showing you the cottage instead. In fact, it's my brother, Keith and I assure you he will offer you the same level of professionalism expected of all the Needham agents. The owner of the cottage has forwarded me the necessary paperwork and Keith will bring everything with him. I apologise again for letting you down but I'm afraid it can't be helped. I'll WhatsApp Keith's mobile number over to you."

"I suppose if it can't be helped, it can't be helped. Is he going to meet us at the cottage?"

"That's right. Do you need directions?"

"We have GPS. We'll find it."

"I'm sure you will, Mrs Green," Darren said. "And if not, the cottage will find you. I believe if a home is meant to be it will be."

They ended the call and Rebecca told Henry what was happening.

"What difference does it make?" Henry said. "I'd prefer to be left in peace entirely while we have a good look at the place anyway. I hate it when there's someone watching over me the whole time. I can't think straight."

"I'm sure Mr Needham's brother will allow us some privacy," Rebecca said. "I just hope we can find the place."

"We'll know it when we see it."

Of this she was convinced. She'd spent hours looking at photos of the cottage on the website and she was sure she had memorised every inch of the place. She would definitely know Sea View Cottage when she saw it.

Henry turned right onto the M27 and the green of the New Forest loomed up ahead.

"Last stretch, love," he said.

"We're not due in Frisk for another three hours," Rebecca said.

"We'll take it slow. The turn-off should be just up ahead somewhere. I'll find some place nice to stop so we can stretch our legs."

"Is your arthritis playing up again?"

"It's not, funnily enough," Henry realised. "Must be because we're getting close to the sea."

At Cadnam they turned left and headed straight into the heart of the New Forest National Park.

"Look at that," Rebecca pointed to the road in front of them.

There was nothing but fields as far as the eye could see. The River Avon ran parallel with the road and every now and again they would find themselves crossing a bridge over it only to cross it again a few miles down the road. It truly was a spectacular scene. A sign on the side of the road told them there was a teahouse up ahead.

"Shall we stop for a bit?" Henry suggested. "We can get a cup of tea and a cake."

"We've got plenty of time," Rebecca said. "And I could drink a nice cup of tea right now."

After a cup of tea and a slice of chocolate cake Rebecca and Henry set off once more.

"There was a sign for Bournemouth back there," Rebecca said. "Should we be heading for Bournemouth?"

"I think I took a wrong turning off the A31," Henry admitted. "It shouldn't take us too far out of our way."

Rebecca brought up the GPS on her phone. "No harm done. Take the next left and we'll be on the coast road on the way to Milford. According to the GPS we'll be able to see the sea soon."

The blue of the Solent came into view a few miles further down the road. It was a glorious early-April day and the sun was high above the Isle of Wight in the distance.

"Sublime," Henry said.

"It's beautiful," Rebecca agreed. "And that's what we're going to be waking up to every morning."

They continued east along the windy coast road. Every now and then a village would appear and Henry slowed down. The sign on the side of the road told him Milford was two miles away.

"It's quiet," Rebecca observed.

"It's Monday," Henry said. "Most people will be at work."

"Half of these places look like nobody lives in them."

"It's Monday, love," Henry said. "Most houses look like this on a Monday."

"I suppose so. I can't wait to get there."

"Not long now."

They reached Frisk ten minutes later. They wouldn't have realised they were there if it wasn't for the GPS. The road sign for the village was filthy and half-obscured by tall grass.

"Here we are," Rebecca said. "Our new home. This feels right – I can feel it in my bones."

"What's the address again?" Henry asked.

"Number 10 Brightwater Lane," Rebecca said. "According to the GPS we take a left up a slight incline and Brightwater Lane is right at the top."

They passed a post office and a quaint-looking pub.

"The Frisk Arms," Henry read. "That could be our new local. Imagine walking down there for Sunday lunch, love."

"This is it," Rebecca said. "Brightwater Lane. Look for number 10."

They didn't have to. There on the right was the reason they were here. Sea View Cottage was exactly as Rebecca had imagined it. The cottage was set back from the road. A well-maintained garden was split in half by a driveway that led to the single garage. The place looked immaculate. A blue BMW was parked outside.

Henry stopped the car behind it and turned off the engine. "What do you think, love?"

Rebecca looked at him with glassy eyes.

"Are you alright?" Henry asked her.

"I am," Rebecca said. "I'm more than alright. It's perfect. Let's buy it."

## CHAPTER SIX

Keith Needham got out of his car when he spotted Rebecca and Henry. Darren's brother wasn't as tall as him and he appeared to have a normal-sized neck. He walked up to the prospective buyers and held out a hand to Henry.

"Keith Needham. How was the drive?"

Henry shook the hand. "We got a bit lost back there but it was worth the detour."

Keith nodded to Rebecca. "Mrs Green. What do you think?"

Rebecca was finding it hard to take in. For once in her life, she was truly lost for words. Her eyes were fixed on the cottage in front of her. There was a signboard behind the wooden gate. *Sea View Cottage* had been written in green italics.

"I imagine you'll want to have a look around," Keith said. "I brought the paperwork with me. You'll be happy to hear the Lawton's have got the ball rolling and it's in the hands of the gods now. Your house is officially sold. Needham's legal team are on it and they'll ensure it's done as quickly as possible, so if you decide you like the cottage, you could be in by next month. How does that sound?"

Rebecca shook her head but she was still unable to speak.

"Let's go and have a look inside, shall we?" Keith said. "I don't usually do this but how about I let you in and leave you be for an hour or so? I imagine you'd like to do this without someone gawping over your shoulder."

"That would be appreciated, Mr Needham," Henry said. "That would be very much appreciated."

Keith unlocked the front door and stepped aside. "I'm going to grab a quick bite to eat at the Frisk Arms. You've got my mobile number – just give me a shout when you're done."

"After you, Mrs Green," Henry said to Rebecca.

The first thing Rebecca noticed when she went inside the cottage was how bright and airy it was inside. The curtains were drawn and the early afternoon sun shone into the living room.

"This is lovely," Rebecca said.

"It's bigger than it looks from outside," Henry noted.

"That's because there's nothing in it. There's no furniture or ornaments or pictures on the wall. It'll be much more homely when we bring our things here."

Her mobile phone started to ring again. She looked at the screen and saw it was Colin's number.

"It's our Col," she said to Henry. "I'll give him a ring when we're finished having a look around. I'm so excited about this."

A short hallway running from the living room led to the kitchen. The wooden fitted cupboards looked new. A large window looked out onto the back garden and the open stretch of ground that was Keyhaven Marshes. Beyond that was the blue of the Solent and further back, the Isle of Wight.

"I love it," Rebecca said. "I absolutely love it. Let's go out to the garden."

"Don't you want to see the bedrooms first?" Henry asked.

"I don't care. I don't care if they're the size of shoeboxes. Look at that view."

She opened the back door and walked outside into the sunshine. Henry followed her.

He looked at the low fence at the very end of the garden. "Foxgloves. I love foxgloves."

"I'm bringing some of my plants here," Rebecca said. "My roses will look lovely there by that rock feature."

"You can't dig up the plants. The old house isn't ours anymore."

"Technically it still is," Rebecca said. "Until the money is in the bank it's still ours."
"The new owners might have something to say about it."
"The Lawtons didn't strike me as the gardening types," Rebecca argued. "They probably won't even notice. Let's sit for a while and enjoy the view."
"It's a beautiful garden," Henry said.
"Someone has put a lot of love into this garden," Rebecca said. "I wonder if someone comes in and looks after it from time to time."
"It looks that way. They probably have a gardener who comes here a couple of days a week. Are those strawberries over there?"
He pointed to a patch of the garden just beyond the kitchen window. Rebecca went to take a look. She bent down and picked two of the plump red fruits and brought them back. She held out her hand to Henry.
He inspected one of the strawberries and popped it in his mouth.
"Juicy and sweet," he said. "I thought they didn't bear fruit until early summer."
"They must be the ever-bearing type," Rebecca said and took a bite of the other strawberry. "Delicious."

In front of the kitchen window was a small veranda with a table and four chairs on it. Rebecca and Henry sat facing the sea. Rebecca closed her eyes and felt the light breeze on her face. When she opened her eyes again, she realised Henry was smiling. He was grinning from ear to ear.
"Can you imagine," he said. "Can you imagine what it's going to be like to come out here every morning with a cup of tea."
"It's going to be like being on holiday every day of the year," Rebecca said. "We've earned this, Henry Green."
"We have, haven't we?"

They sat there for quite some time, neither of them speaking. There was nothing to say. Nothing could describe that moment in the garden of Sea

View Cottage. A sound from next door broke their reverie. It was the sound of breaking glass.

"What was that?" Henry said.

"It sounded like it came from next door," Rebecca said.

Henry stood up and stretched his arms wide. The drive to Frisk was starting to take its toll on his arthritic joints. He walked over to the low wall that separated number 10 from number 12. A middle-aged man was throwing empty bottles into a wheelie bin.

"Hello there," Henry shouted to him. "Have a bit of a knees-up last night, did you?"

The man looked over but didn't return the greeting. He finished emptying the bottles and walked inside the house without saying a word.

"Friendly chap," Henry said to Rebecca. "Shall we go and see the rest of the cottage now?"

The main bedroom was at the end of the hallway. It was roughly the same size as their bedroom back in Wimbledon. The view from here was just as spectacular as the view from the garden. The second bedroom was smaller but they would easily be able to fit a double bed inside.

"This can be the guest bedroom," Rebecca said. "For when the kids and grandkids come to stay."

The third bedroom looked onto the front garden. It was quite small and offered merely a view of the garden and the road at the end.

"We can use this as a study," Rebecca suggested. "We can put the computer and your books in here."

"We should get one of those sofa beds," Henry pointed to the wall opposite the window. "We can use it when the twins stay over."

The bathroom also had a sea view. Henry was starting to have doubts about changing the name of the cottage. Sea View Cottage really was a fitting name.

They spent the next half-an-hour inspecting the cottage. Rebecca was opening and closing cupboards and drawers in the kitchen and Henry was designing his study in his head. He heard the sound of a car door slamming outside. He looked out of the window and watched as a white Ford van sped away. There was a sign on the side of the van – Henry couldn't quite make out what it said but it looked like a sticker for a cleaning company.

He found Rebecca in the main bedroom. She was sitting on the bed and she was crying. Tears were rolling down her cheeks.

Henry sat down next to her. "What's up, love?"

Rebecca wiped her face. "Nothing. Absolutely nothing. I just felt so happy I needed to cry. I'm sorry."

Henry shook his head. "Women."

"Shall we do this, Henry?" Rebecca asked him. "Shall we buy the place?"

"I think that might be a very good idea," Henry said. "Get hold of that estate agent and let's sign those damn papers."

# CHAPTER SEVEN

The drive back to London passed in silence. Returning to Wimbledon seemed somewhat anticlimactic after the trip to Frisk. Even the weather seemed to be playing along – they'd driven thirty miles up the M3 when the heavens opened.

"Typical."

Henry eased his foot off the accelerator and turned on the windscreen wipers.

They'd called Keith Needham and told him they were ready to sign the necessary paperwork. Both Rebecca and Henry had been surprised at just how much paperwork there was to get through. Keith had told them most of it was self-explanatory and to ask him if there was anything they didn't understand. Rebecca's hand ached when they were finished. She'd never written her initials on so many sheets of paper before and she was glad when they reached the last page.

It was out of their hands now – all they could do was wait. Keith had explained the procedure in some detail. Needham Properties would be handling everything. As soon as the sale of the house in Wimbledon went through the funds would sit in the bank account of the lawyers until such time as the sale of Sea View Cottage was finalised. Keith assured Rebecca and Henry they didn't need to worry about a thing. Sea View Cottage was as good as theirs. What Keith neglected to mention was the commission from the sale of the two properties would net Needham Properties close to a hundred-thousand-pounds. Not bad for a few days' work.

The rain eased off a bit as the Greens passed underneath the M25 and continued north.

"Is it just me," Rebecca said. "Or does London seem more grim and depressing today?"

They were on the M3 heading north and the skyline of the city in front of them looked grey and dismal. The tops of the skyscrapers were covered in a blanket of dark cloud.

"It's always been grim, love," Henry said. "It looks worse today because we're on the way back from Frisk. It won't be for long."

Rebecca's phone started to ring. The screen told her it was Colin again. She'd forgotten about returning his call when they became engrossed in signing the necessary documents to secure Sea View Cottage.

"Hello, love," Rebecca answered the call. "Sorry I didn't phone you back – we were busy with the cottage."

"You haven't signed anything, have you?" Colin asked.

"We signed the contract Mr Needham spoke of yesterday. You should see the place, Col, the photos don't do it justice. It's perfect and there's no work needs doing on it. We're going to buy it. Hold on, I'll put us on speaker so your dad can hear us."

The line went quiet for a while and Rebecca wondered if she'd accidentally ended the call.

"Are you still there?" she asked.

"I'm still here. You shouldn't have been so hasty," Colin said.

"You said it was fine yesterday. You were the one who set the terms and conditions."

"I'd had a bit to drink. I wasn't thinking straight, but when I thought about it today, I realised I'd been taken for a fool. Needham Properties will speed up the sale of your house and they're going to make damn sure the deal goes through before the three weeks is over."

"I don't like it when you swear, love. What's the problem? Your father and me love the place – the quicker the better if you ask me."

"I had a bit of spare time at the office today," Colin said. "So, I did a bit of digging into the area."

"It's a peaceful, safe, tranquil area. We saw that for ourselves today. There's nothing to worry about."

"A lot of the houses in Frisk stand empty for most of the week."

"Then it'll be even quieter. Loads of people have second homes - somewhere they can come to get away from the stress of the city."

"They're not holiday homes, mum. Most of them are holiday rentals. The owners rent them out for weekends and holidays."

"I still can't see what the problem is, Col," Rebecca said. "Who cares if people want to go on holiday? It's a beautiful place to go on holiday."

"There's this company called HomeFromHome," Colin continued. "It's become very popular recently and for a small fee homeowners can list their houses on its website. Anyone these days can rent out their house to anyone they want."

"Good luck to them, I say," Henry joined in.

"You don't know how many complaints these HomeFromHome rentals have received, dad," Colin said. "It's turning into a real problem. The guests these holidays rentals attract can often be less than desirable. For a few quid you can enjoy a house by the sea. And very often the guests turn out to be a real nuisance to the neighbours nearby. I'm just telling you what I've read."

"I still can't see how it's going to affect us," Rebecca said. "If we get noisy guests next door, we'll just ask them to keep it down a bit."

"I'm just looking out for you, mum."

"And I appreciate it, love."

"I think that's why the cottage is so cheap," Colin said. "I think the owner wanted a quick sale to get the hell away from the nuisance guests."

"You're being overdramatic now, son," Henry said. "We're almost home. We'll chat later. You've got nothing to worry about."

"I'll take a look at this HomeFromHome thing," Rebecca assured him. "But I can't see it being a problem."

The rain had eased off a bit as they turned into their street and drove towards the house. Black smoke was drifting across the road from the house belonging to Mr and Mrs Havisham and as they got closer Henry realised Mr Havisham had finally brought the old camper van back to life. He was working on the engine at the back of the van. Every now and then another cloud of noxious black smoke would explode from the exhaust and rise up into the air. Henry couldn't remember how long the old rust-bucket had been parked across the road but it had been a very long time.

"Typical," Henry said as he and Rebecca got out of the car. "Just as we're about to move, old Havisham decides to fix his van."

"He'd better watch out," Rebecca said. "Mr Finch at number 22 will report him to the council if he carries on polluting the air like that."

"Let him," Henry said. "I never had much time for those Havishams. Shall I put the kettle on?"

"That would be lovely. It's been a long day. Shall we order a takeaway for tea?"

"Sounds like a plan," Henry agreed. "I quite fancy a Chinese."

# CHAPTER EIGHT

Rebecca cleared away the empty food cartons and turned on the kettle to make some tea. Alfred was polishing off a bowl of food next to the back door and Henry was reading a book in the living room. The phone call with Colin had made Rebecca uneasy and she planned on spending the evening putting her mind at rest. She knew her son's intentions were good but there was something in the undertones of what he'd spoken about that unnerved her.

She took the two cups of tea through to the living room and handed one to Henry.

He looked up from his book. "Thanks, love. I'm struggling with this one."

Rebecca looked at the cover. "Around the World in 80 Plays? Sounds very highbrow."

"It's not," Henry said and took a sip of his tea. "It's rather pedestrian to be honest. The premise looked promising – I was intrigued at how Greenbow – that's the author, was going to put it all together. I suppose the whole idea was pretty risky. Travelling the world looking for the settings from eighty plays was bound to become stale sooner or later. There are only so many ways to describe a scene from a play in a modern context. And the subheadings are a tad trite if you ask me."

"You don't have to finish it," Rebecca told him.

"I paid for it," Henry said. "I'm going to finish the damn thing."

"I'm going to do some research on that HomeFromHome company," Rebecca said and placed her laptop on the coffee table. "I want to see for myself if these holiday rentals are as bad as our Colin made out."

"He's just being overly cautious," Henry said. "He's an accountant – they're all like that."

"I want to see what it's all about, anyway."

"Much Ado About Nothing," Henry read the heading at the top of the page. "That pretty much sums up the content of this book."

"You don't have to read it if you don't like it," Rebecca told him once more.

"I'm finishing it. I've never not finished a book."

"Could you keep your pedantic disapproval to yourself, though?" Rebecca asked him. "I'd quite like to do this in peace."

Henry didn't reply. He carried on reading his book, shaking his head as he did so.

Rebecca found the HomeFromHome website without too much trouble. She had to admit it did look very professional. The home page had clearly been designed by someone who knew what they were doing. It was striking and caught the eye immediately. There was a list of options at the top of the page.

Location, checking in date, number of nights, and number of guests were written in block capitals. At the side of the page was an option to *Become a HomeFromHome host*. There were also links to how HomeFromHome works and a list of their policies and rules.

Rebecca typed *Frisk* in the space next to *Location* and selected some random dates and said she wanted a house for two adults. She was shocked at what appeared next on the screen. Colin hadn't been exaggerating – there were thirteen listings for the small village of Frisk alone. Thirteen homes in the village Rebecca and Henry were planning on moving to were being used by their owners as a source of income via HomeFromHome. Photographs of the holiday homes appeared on the left of the screen. Rebecca scrolled down and her eyes fell on something very familiar. It looked like the cottage next door to Sea View Cottage.

This was confirmed when Rebecca clicked on it. The address at the bottom was number 12 Brightwater Lane. There were more photographs as well as a list of amenities, things to do in the area and a calendar showing the dates still available to rent the cottage. Rebecca gasped when she realised the cottage next door to the one she and Henry had agreed to buy was booked for every weekend in the foreseeable future. Every Saturday and Sunday was crossed out right up until the end of August. The upcoming Easter weekend was booked from the Thursday to the Monday.

"Colin was right," Rebecca told Henry. "The cottage next door to Sea View Cottage is a HomeFromHome rental. That's probably what that man was doing earlier - he was cleaning up the empties after a boozy weekend."

Henry put down his book. "Do you think we ought to reconsider?"

"I don't think we can. We've signed a contract."

"There's always ways of getting out of a contract."

"I loved that cottage," Rebecca said. "Surely it can't be that bad having a holiday rental next door."

"This HomeFromHome company must have some rules," Henry said. "There must be a list of rules about being considerate to the permanent residents."

There was. It was a very long list and as Rebecca read the guidelines about taking the residents in the surrounding houses into account, she felt somewhat relieved.

"They seem to have strong policies on residential disturbances," she told Henry. "There are strict rules about parties and loud noise. And there's a support centre where you can report neighbourhood concerns."

"I just don't want to be lumbered with a cottage that backs onto a nightclub at the weekends," Henry said.

"Don't be daft. The guests are not allowed to make too much noise. And the sort of people who go to a place like Frisk wouldn't go there to disrupt the village. It'll probably be mostly families with kids who'll spend the whole day at the beach."

"I suppose you're right," Henry said. "Do you think giraffe-neck from the estate agents knew about these HomeFromHome rentals?"

"Why would he?"

"I'd have thought it would be his job to know. And if he did know, why didn't he mention it?"

"Perhaps he didn't think it was important. I'm sure an estate agent has an obligation to inform a potential buyer about something that might affect their quality of life. You heard what Darren Needham said about integrity."

"Nonsense. Estate agents are only interested in one thing. Their commission. They'll stoop to any level to sell a house and that Darren Needham looks like he's capable of stooping lower than most."

"Colin is just looking out for us," Rebecca insisted. "Everything has happened so quickly and he's just doing what any concerned son would do. I really don't think we have anything to worry about. Buying Sea View Cottage is going to be the best thing we've ever done."

Henry looked up from his book. Something in the tone of his wife's voice seemed slightly off. The change was a subtle one but Henry was sure he detected a hint of doubt in her words and he wondered if they were about to make the biggest mistake of their lives. He pushed the idea aside and turned his attention back to the book. Graham Greenbow had arrived in Seville and was planning on getting a haircut there. Henry read half of the first page of the new chapter then threw the book on the coffee table so violently it almost knocked his tea flying.

Rebecca looked at him and smiled. "Is it that bad?"

"I can't read any more," Henry said. "Life is far too short to waste time on drivel like this."

## CHAPTER NINE

The following week flew by in a blur of packing and ticking things off lists. Rebecca had been a maker of lists for as long as Henry could remember. It was a running joke in the family. Rebecca made lists for everything under the sun. Henry couldn't remember a time when there wasn't a sheet of paper stuck to the fridge with a list of things that needed doing on it. More often than not, the list would remain unchecked. There was always something new to be added to that list.

Piles of boxes were stacked in every room. Alfred hadn't enjoyed the packing at all – the wily Jack Russell sensed something was about to happen and he was clearly not happy about it. When Rebecca had taken the extra bedding out of the wardrobe in the spare room and piled it on the floor, the dog had taken up residence on top and refused to budge. In the end Henry had to manhandle him and frog-march him out of the room so Rebecca could work in peace.

"We're going to need more boxes," Henry shouted from his study. Rebecca was going through a checklist of things that could be safely packed – things they could do without until they moved to the cottage.

"What was that?" she shouted back.

"More boxes," Henry replied. "We're going to need more boxes – I didn't realise how many books I actually had in here."

Rebecca appeared in the doorway, list in hand. "Do you really need to take all of them? There must be books in here you haven't looked at in years."

"It's that old enigma," Henry said. "As soon as you chuck something out, even after years and years of not using it, you suddenly need it. I don't want to find myself in that kind of quandary."

"Why don't you get a Kindle?" Rebecca suggested. "I've been telling you for years you should get a Kindle. You can get all of these on one small device."

"Sorry, love," Henry picked up a tattered paperback. "There are memories in every single one of these. I can't bear to leave any of them behind."

Rebecca sighed. She knew arguing about this was futile. "We can see if Mrs Hall from the corner shop can give us some more boxes."

"How are you getting on?" Henry asked.

"Getting there slowly. There's a lot more to pack than I thought. You realise we're going to have to make a decision about what we're going to take and what we're going to give away or take to the charity shop. The cottage is quite a bit smaller than this place and we won't be able to fit everything in."

Henry nodded. "It is surprising how much a person accumulates over the years."

"We can't take it all, Henry."

"I know. I'll make you a deal – you let me keep my books and I'll leave it up to you to decide what we take and what we don't."

Rebecca knew this was a very good deal. She'd also predicted her husband would make this kind of deal and as such, she'd already prepared a list consisting of four columns.

*Things to take with them to Sea View Cottage.*

*Things to offer to Colin and Phoebe.*

*Things to take to the charity shop.*

The fourth column was the hardest of all to think about. In this column were the possessions that Rebecca intended to throw away. These were items that she knew would be no use to anyone. It was a difficult decision to make but sometimes a person just needed to take a leap of faith and let go. In the end Rebecca convinced herself it was time to put the old memories behind her and concentrate on all the new ones she and Henry were about to make at Sea View Cottage.

It was just after two in the afternoon and Rebecca and Henry were taking a well-earned tea break when the doorbell rang.

"I'll get it," Henry offered.

He eased himself up from his armchair and went to see who it was. Alfred followed after him.

Darren Needham was grinning from ear to ear. The Jack Russel started to growl.

"That's enough, Alfred," Henry said.

"Mr Green," Darren said. "Sorry to barge in unannounced but I thought I'd come and see you in person."

"Is there something wrong?"

"On the contrary," Darren said. "Is Mrs Green home?"

Alfred was now growling non-stop. He bared his teeth and started to bark.

"Come in," Henry said. "Kettle's just boiled."

"Could you do something about the dog?" Darren said. "He seems to have taken a bit of a dislike to me."

*He's not the only one,* Henry thought.

They sat in the living room. Henry had persuaded Alfred to go outside to the back garden with the help of a small plate of leftover chicken.

"What's happened?" Rebecca came straight to the point.

"I don't normally do this in person," Darren said. "But I thought, as I was in the area I'd come and give you the good news in person."

"Good news?" Henry said.

"I'm sure you're aware that the Lawton's have transferred the money for your house over to the solicitors."

"I got a message about it on Monday," Rebecca told him.

"That's right. The final steps in the conveyancing process were set in motion the moment the funds cleared."

"I'm not following you," Henry said.

"It basically means the time to move is fast approaching, Mr Green."
"We haven't finished packing," Rebecca told him.
"Don't worry, we're not talking about hours here. I estimate you will be able to move into Sea View Cottage before the end of the month."
"There's still a lot to organise," Henry said. "We haven't even got quotes from removal companies."
"I can point you in the direction of a few reputable ones," Darren offered. "But in the meantime, I've been in contact with the lawyers handling the estate of Mrs Wright – she's the previous owner of Sea View Cottage and they've agreed it shouldn't be a problem for you to start moving bits and bobs in right away. That way when the final moving day does arrive, it won't be so stressful."
"That sounds like a good idea," Henry said.
"Estate?" Rebecca said. "You said you've spoken to Mrs Wright's lawyers. You didn't mention she was dead. In fact, I seem to remember you saying something about her not being unreasonable."
"You must have misheard me," Darren said. "Needham Properties have been dealing with the lawyers handling the estate all along. I'm sure I told you that."
"You bloody well did not." It was Henry.
"Henry," Rebecca said. "Don't be rude."

"Let's calm down a bit," Darren said. "I think this has just been a bit of a misunderstanding. And I apologise if I didn't make it clear the sale of Sea View Cottage is through a deceased estate. However, it doesn't make a blind bit of difference to you, as the buyers. In fact, the headache is all Needham's – we are handling the nitty-gritty and we aim to make this as painless as possible for you."

"You say we can start moving stuff to the cottage right away?" Henry asked.

"I couldn't help but notice you've made quite a bit of headway with the packing," Darren said. "I would suggest you start moving possessions you can live without for a week or two. Things that will fit in the boot of the car."

"We can take your books," Rebecca suggested. "We can ask Colin and Phoebe to help us. Colin has a load of space in that people-carrier of his and the kids and grandkids can see the cottage at the same time."

"Sounds like a plan," Henry agreed. "We can make a whole weekend of it."

Darren Needham raised his hand in the air to get their attention.

"The weekend is out of the question, I'm afraid."

"It's the only time the kids will be able to help," Rebecca said. "Colin and Phoebe both work during the week."

"Unfortunately, this weekend isn't convenient."

"Why not?' Henry asked.

"The lawyers handling the estate made it quite clear a representative of Needham Properties is to accompany you and I'm afraid all our agents are busy this weekend. Monday will work."

"I don't get it," Henry said. "Why can't you just give us the keys? It's not like we're going to steal something from a cottage we've all but bought."

"That's not the problem, Mr Green. Like I said, Mrs Wright's lawyers are not being unreasonable, but I suggest you meet them halfway. You will only be able to start moving in during the week.'

The room fell silent for a moment. Alfred started to bark outside in the back garden.

"Something doesn't feel right here." Rebecca was the first to speak.

"I assure you everything is above board, Mrs Green," Darren said.

"Why are you so determined to keep us away from the cottage at the weekend? What exactly happens in Frisk over the weekend?"

"I'm not sure I follow you."

"Is there something you haven't told us?" Henry added.

"I've been straight-up with you every step of the way, Mr Green. I really have to get going – I have a meeting with a client in ten minutes and I'm probably going to be late. Someone from the office will be in touch over the weekend to make the necessary arrangements."

Rebecca wasn't quite sure how long she and Henry sat in silence after Darren Needham had gone but when she picked up her tea, she realised it had gone cold. Her stomach was growling at her and it wasn't because she was hungry. Something deep down inside her was sending out a warning that something was wrong.

Something was terribly wrong.

## CHAPTER TEN

"Where did you put the tongs?" Henry shouted through the open kitchen window.

He'd decided to organise a last-minute barbecue. The weather forecast looked good for the whole weekend and reality was starting to hit home – their days in the house they'd called home for over forty years were coming to an end. Phoebe and her new boyfriend, Len were coming over as were Colin, Susan and the twins. Mr and Mrs Duncan from next door said they would pop in later. Henry had lit the barbecue and the smell of smoke was drifting up into the air.

"They're already packed," Rebecca shouted back. "You're only making burgers and sausages - you can flip them with a fork."

She came outside with the dish containing the meat. It was just after noon and it was promising to be a glorious early-April day.

The anxiety she'd felt after the conversation with Darren Needham was still lingering in the pit of her stomach and she hoped the barbecue would help to take her mind of things. She hadn't been able to sleep last night. Something in the words Darren had spoken sounded warning bells she wasn't able to ignore.

Why was he so keen to keep them away from the cottage at the weekend? Did something happen on Saturdays and Sundays he didn't want them to know about?

Rebecca couldn't for the life of her figure out what that could be. It didn't make any sense. Surely Darren Needham realised they would be moving to the cottage permanently – they would be there seven-days-a-week, but still Rebecca couldn't shake the feeling that something wasn't quite right.

The sound of the doorbell interrupted her thoughts and Rebecca went to see who it was. She was surprised when she opened the door and found Mr and Mrs Havisham from across the road standing there. Rebecca didn't mind Arnold and Zoe but for some reason Henry had never warmed to them. They'd moved in almost twenty years ago and Henry had barely spoken two words to them in that time. He particularly disliked Arnold's arrogance and his manner of speaking.

"Sorry to bother you," Zoe said.

She was a timid woman in her early fifties. Her mousy-brown hair always looked unwashed and her eyes wouldn't keep still. They darted back and forth as though she was expecting an ambush at any time. She was constantly apologising. Rebecca had often wondered if Arnold abused her behind closed doors.

"We heard you was moving," Arnold said. "And we came to see if the rumours was true."

Rebecca was suddenly glad it was she who'd answered the door and not Henry.

"The rumours are true," she said. "We've found a lovely cottage looking out to the Isle of Wight."

"That must've cost you a bob or two," Arnold said.

"We've been putting a bit aside every month."

"Is that a barbie I can smell? Lovely day for it. We was planning on doing the same. Seems a shame to waste this weather. Although Zoe and me are on our own. Seems a shame for us to be barbecuing on our own."

As subtle hints went, Rebecca thought this was one of the worst she'd ever heard. She knew Henry would be annoyed if she invited the Havishams to join them, but it wouldn't be long before they never had to see them again so Rebecca decided to be charitable.

"Would you like to join us?"

"We'd love to," Zoe squeaked. "Sorry – we didn't mean to be rude."

"We don't want to impose," Arnold added.

Henry's face told a story of its own when he realised they were going to have uninvited guests from across the road. Arnold had helped himself to a beer from the kitchen and he and Zoe had gone outside into the back garden.

"Why did you invite them?" Henry asked Rebecca.

"They invited themselves," Rebecca said. "I could hardly tell them to bugger off."

"I would have done."

"I know you would. Come on, love, we're only going to be here for another week or two – let's try and be nice."

"I'll try," Henry said. "But I'm not promising anything. Did they even bring meat?"

Rebecca nodded to a clingfilm-wrapped carton containing two small lamb chops.

"Well, they'd better leave my burgers alone."

Colin, Susan and the twins arrived the same time as Phoebe and Len. Rebecca and Henry hadn't yet met Phoebe's new boyfriend. In fact, Henry had all but given up bothering to remember his daughter's boyfriend's names. Phoebe was almost forty but she'd never had much luck with men.

Katie and Paul were halfway up the stairs when Susan's voice stopped them in their tracks. The twins were running on auto-pilot and were making a beeline for the PC in the spare bedroom.

"Not today," Susan told them. "Your nan and your granddad will be moving soon and we won't see so much of them after that. It's a lovely day today, and the fresh air will do you good."

"Mum," the twins protested in unison.

"Get down here right now," Colin told them. "Aunt Phoebe hasn't seen you for ages. No computer today."

The twins looked at each other and reluctantly stomped back down the stairs.

Susan joined Rebecca in the kitchen. "Is there anything I can help you with?"

"I'm fine, thanks, love," Rebecca said. "The salads done and Henry is taking care of the meat."

"I bet you're all excited about the move. I can't wait to see the cottage."

"I'm starting to wonder if we're doing the right thing," Rebecca said.

"Of course you are. It's only natural to get a bit emotional after all these years in Wimbledon. It'll be nice to get away from London."

"I suppose so. It's just something's bothering me about the whole thing. Something is chewing at my insides telling me something isn't quite right. I can't quite put my finger on it but it's like it's too good to be true."

"You deserve it," Susan said. "You both deserve it."

"Have you met Phoebe's latest?" Rebecca changed the subject.

"He seems nice," Susan said. "He looks quite a bit younger than her though. And he's a lot more respectable than some of the others."

"I give up with that girl. What's his name again?"

"Len. He works over in Streatham."

"Streatham? Do you know what he does?"

"I think Phoebe said he's an estate agent."

"God help us all," Rebecca said. "I just hope my Henry doesn't get wind of that."

# CHAPTER ELEVEN

"Barbecue's almost done," Henry announced.

"Those burgers look raw to me," Arnold Havisham observed.

Arnold had taken it upon himself to supervise the cooking of the meat and Henry hadn't been able to get rid of him. The VW van owner from across the road had managed to drink his way through a six-pack of Henry's lager and Henry was on the verge of telling him to leave when Colin came to the rescue.

"I left my phone in the car," he said. "And when I went to get it, I noticed a bunch of kids hanging around the camper van."

"What?" Arnold said.

"They were probably just admiring it," Colin carried on. "But they looked like they were up to no good to me."

"Bastards."

With that, Arnold swigged the rest of the beer in his can and hurried inside the house.

"Thanks, son," Henry said. "I'm not predisposed to violence but Arnold Havisham is enough to make anyone reconsider. Do those burgers look raw to you?"

"They look almost done. Mum told us about the deceased estate. I didn't know the cottage was part of a deceased estate."

"Us neither. The slimy estate agent reckons he mentioned it but your mother and I know for a fact he didn't. Needham said it won't make any difference to us."

"When are you planning on moving?"

"We can start taking small things to the cottage on Monday," Henry said. "We were hoping to do it this weekend but we were told not to. It would have been easier with you and Phoebe helping out."

"Why couldn't you start this weekend?"
"That's something that's starting to bother us, son. Darren Needham is doing everything he can to keep us from going to the cottage at the weekend. It's like something happens down there on Saturday and Sunday, he doesn't want us to know about."
"Do you think it's something to do with the HomeFromHome next door?"

Henry didn't have the chance to reply to this. A very red-faced Arnold Havisham appeared. He'd brought some more lagers outside.
"There was nobody there. The kids must have legged it."
"I made a point of making my presence known," Colin told him. "I probably scared them off."
"I appreciate it. What have I missed?"
"Nothing much," Colin said. "We were just talking about the move to the coast."
"Do you need some help? I've got the old camper up and running again and there's loads of room in the back. It'll do her good to get a run out."
Henry thought about this for a split second and decided he would rather walk the eighty-odd-miles to Frisk with his belongings on his back than have to endure the trip with Arnold Havisham.
"Thanks for the offer," he said. "But we've got it all organised.
"Removal companies are rip-offs," Arnold wasn't quite finished yet. "I've got a mate who can do you a good deal. He needs the work."
*And there's probably a good reason for that*, Henry thought.
"Thanks for the offer, but we've got it covered. I'd say that meat is done."

They ate from paper plates. Rebecca apologised for it but nobody complained. Arnold Havisham excused himself from the barbecue as soon as he'd finished the last morsel of food on his plate. Zoe was forced to wolf down the rest of hers under her husband's disapproving gaze.
"Spurs are playing in half an hour," Arnold said. "It should be a blinder."

"How rude," Susan said when the Havishams had gone. "That man has the manners of an ape."

"Good riddance to him," Henry said.

"Spurs aren't playing until tomorrow," Phoebe's boyfriend, Len pointed out. "They're playing Huddersfield at home."

"He just used that as an excuse so he could leave," Susan added. "What a horrible man."

"I don't care what his excuse was," Henry said. "I was this close to fetching the axe from the shed."

"We hadn't thought about the shed," Rebecca said. "We've been so busy packing up things in the house, we forgot about the tools in the shed."

"It's on the list," Henry said and tapped his head.

Katie and Paul had appeared next to them. Henry hadn't even realised the twins were there. They both looked annoyed at having to miss out on valuable computer time.

"Why don't you two get off upstairs," Rebecca told them. "But before you go, come and give your old nan a hug.

They reluctantly obliged and as Rebecca embraced them, she slid something into the hands of both of them. Katie opened her fist and stared at the crumpled five-pound-note. Paul looked at his as though it were a shrivelled-up slug.

"What do you say?" Susan said to them.

"Thanks, nan," Paul spoke first.

"Thanks, nan," Katie echoed.

"Off you go then," Rebecca said.

"I sometimes wonder about them," Colin said. "They're like teenagers already."

"Nonsense," Susan said. "They're only nine."

"Did you see their faces when they saw the fivers?" Phoebe joined in.

"I suppose five-pounds isn't what it used to be," Rebecca said.

"They've both got such intense stares," Phoebe said and nudged Colin in the side. "You need to be very afraid, brother of mine. They might seem like cute little nine-year-old kids on the outside, but deep down something sinister is brewing. That's how the Kray twins started out."

"Very funny." Colin was clearly not amused by his sister's remark. "I'm going to get another drink. Can I get anyone else one?"

"I'll have a lager if Arnold Havisham hasn't finished them all," Henry said.

"Do you need help with the dishes, mum," Phoebe offered.

"There aren't many, love," Rebecca said. "We're not going to wash paper plates, are we? But you can give me a hand with the glasses and cutlery."

Phoebe kissed Henry on the top of the head. "Thanks for the barbecue, dad."

"I'll give you a hand," Susan said and followed Rebecca and Phoebe inside the house.

## CHAPTER TWELVE

Henry was left alone with Phoebe's boyfriend. Henry wasn't one for small talk and the two men stood in awkward silence for a while.

"Phoebe said you're moving down to the coast," Len said eventually.

"That's right," was all Henry felt like telling him.

"Down by Milford?"

"It's a place called Frisk. The cottage looks out onto the Isle of Wight. We got it for a song."

"Why was it so cheap?"

"The owner wanted a quick sale, I suppose," Henry said. "Everything happened so fast, and the agent was a bit pushy for my liking. I have an inbuilt mistrust of estate agents."

Len laughed. "You're dead right there. Some of us are very shifty."

"Some of us...?"

"Phoebe didn't tell you what I do for a living, did she, Mr Green."

"Mrs Green always said that one day I will stick my foot so far in my mouth, it will be impossible to retrieve. I apologise if I've offended you."

"No offence taken," Len said. "I agree with you. I'm thinking of getting out of the industry anyway – it's dog-eat-dog out there and I'm not cut out for it."

"How long have you been an estate agent?"

"Five years. I was laid off when the recruitment agency I was working for went under and a friend said there was money in selling property. How is everything going with the move?"

Henry thought hard for a moment. He wasn't sure if he could trust this man enough to confide in him his concerns about the move to Sea View Cottage.

"How did you and Phoebe meet?" he asked instead.

"I was on a night out at this place on the King's Road," Len said. "When Phoebe and some other women walked in. We got chatting and I liked her honesty."

"Our Phoebe does call a spade a spade," Henry agreed. "It's got her into trouble quite a few times, I don't mind telling you."

"We hit it off, and here we are."

"She's had her fair share of problems," Henry said. "But she's a strong one."

"I know all about the drugs," Len said. "Like I said, Phoebe isn't shy with the truth, and I suppose everyone is entitled to a past, however dark that past might be."

"There is one thing that's bothering me and Mrs Green about the move to Frisk," Henry decided to come out with it. "We weren't told we would be moving next door to a HomeFromHome rental."

"You should have been informed," Len said.

"The estate agent neglected to mention it. And something else we've found odd is he has been reluctant to let us anywhere near the cottage at the weekend. It's like there's something that happens there he doesn't want us to see. I'm starting to think the HomeFromHome next door could be a real problem."

"I don't know much about these weekend rentals," Len said. "But they normally don't allow the guests to make a nuisance of themselves. HomeFromHome is a big operation, and they'll have measures in place to prevent the people renting out the properties from having a negative impact on the residents nearby. If there is a problem the seller has an obligation to mention it in the initial conveyancing questionnaires."

"The seller is dead," Henry told him.

"It doesn't matter. Then it lies with the lawyers representing the deceased estate. You should have received this documentation."

"What if we didn't?"

"Then, if the seller or the agent representing the seller neglected to inform you of something of this nature, the contract could be deemed null and void."

This was all a bit much for Henry to take in. He'd always considered himself a cut above the rest where the English language was concerned but legalese always baffled him in its complexity. He'd always maintained that the language of the law was designed to keep lawyers in employment - they were the only ones who could make any sense out of it.

"I can have a quick look at the documents you and Mrs Green signed," Len offered.

"I'd appreciate that," Henry said. "I don't know why lawyers can't just communicate in plain English."

Colin came back out with Phoebe. He handed Henry and Len a can of lager each.

"Glad to see you two are still in one piece," Phoebe said to Henry and Len.

"He's not too bad," Henry said, then added, "for an estate agent."

"I said I'd have a quick look at the papers they signed for the cottage," Len said. "Just to put their minds at rest."

Phoebe rested her head on her father's shoulders. "I knew you two would get on - I just knew it."

Henry decided it would be best to go through the contract they'd signed at the kitchen table. Len sat in between him and Rebecca and Colin, Phoebe and Susan sat opposite them. The twins were still engrossed in their computer game upstairs.

Len took out a pair of reading glasses and put them on. "This looks like a standard draft contract. Hold on. This is odd."

Rebecca froze. "What's odd?"

"It's nothing to worry about but the TA6, TA10 and TA13 have been included."

"In English please, Len." It was Phoebe.

"Sorry," Len said. "Usually, these documents aren't there for the buyer to view – they form the basis of the contract the conveyancer draws up, but in this instance they're all there."

"What exactly does that mean?" Henry asked.

"Sorry," Len said. "The TA13 includes the nitty-gritty. Stuff like when occupation will take place and the handing over of keys, as well as confirming the property is free of mortgages and liabilities. The T10 pertains to agreements such as which fixtures and fittings will be sold with the property. It all seems to be in order. It appears the estate agent you went with has offered you absolute transparency."

"That's good to hear," Henry said.

"What about the other document?" Rebecca said. "You mentioned another one."

"Oh yes," Len said. "The TA6. That's just a basic questionnaire asking about general neighbourhood things. Border disputes and building works and the like. Oh. This isn't good."

"What isn't good?" Rebecca said.

"I need to check something."

Len flipped through the main contract until he found what he was looking for.

"You both signed this."

"We signed the whole lot," Henry told him.

"What's wrong?" Phoebe said.

"In the TA6 questionnaire it clearly mentions the HomeFromHome rental next door. It also points out that that one isn't the only holiday rental on Brightwater Lane."

"But we already knew that," Henry said.

"What you didn't know is there have been numerous complaints from residents on Brightwater Lane about the nuisance these weekend rentals have become. Rowdy behaviour, noise pollution, not to mention occasional threats against residents."

"But they didn't sign anything acknowledging they were informed of this," Colin argued. "They can use that to get out of the deal. If they'd known about the noisy guests, they never would have agreed to buy the cottage."

Len slid the contract across the table to him. Right there in black and white on the page containing the disclosure about the neighbourhood complaints were Colin's parents' initials. Rebecca and Henry had signed without realising what they had signed. There was nothing they could do about it now – the moment they put pen to paper they'd committed to buying Sea View Cottage.

## CHAPTER THIRTEEN

Colin arrived the next morning with a bald man in his mid-fifties. The upbeat atmosphere of the barbecue had vanished when Rebecca and Henry realised they were bound by the contract they'd signed to buy Sea View Cottage and both of them felt like their dream property was quickly turning into the stuff of nightmares.

Colin introduced the man as Greg Higgins. He was a lawyer the accounting firm Colin worked for used from time to time. Greg was so thin it was bordering on malnutrition. His thick glasses made his eyes seem much larger than they were.

"Thank you for seeing us on a Sunday," Rebecca said. "I'll put the kettle on."

Henry led Greg and Colin into the living room and they sat down.

"Colin has outlined your problem, Mr Green," Greg said. "Do you mind if I take a look through the contract you and Mrs Green signed?"

"I'll go and get it," Henry said.

He returned with Rebecca. She placed a tray of tea and biscuits on the table.

Henry handed the contract to Greg.

"I'll pour the tea," Rebecca said.

"This is a standard contract," Greg said after a few minutes. "The lawyers representing the estate and the agents selling the property haven't done anything untoward."

"But we weren't told about the noisy guests," Henry told him.

"According to this, you were."

"We didn't see that part," Rebecca said.

"It doesn't matter," Greg said. "You signed it."

"Isn't there anything they can do about it?" Colin asked. "Surely they can't be forced to buy a property."

"The only way to get out of it is to be in breach of contract," Greg said. "And with that comes a whole load of problems. I believe this house has been sold?"

"The buyer's money is in the lawyer's account," Rebecca said.

"Then not only would you be facing the penalties incurred with the breach on the Sea View Cottage deal, but you would have to find somewhere else to live very quickly."

"What are the penalties?" Henry asked. "For breach of contract?"

"Best case scenario," Greg said. "Is you'd have to fork out the commission due to the estate agent."

"And the worst-case scenario?" Rebecca said.

"The lawyers representing the deceased estate could sue you for breach of contract and that could cost you a lot of money."

"What do you suggest we do?" Henry said.

"My advice to you would be this," Greg said. "Carry on as planned. Move to Sea View Cottage and see how it goes. If these HomeFromHome rentals do turn out to be problematic, you can always sell the place again. I believe you got it for a really good price."

"Probably because nobody wants to live in a place that turns into a nightclub at weekends," Henry said.

"You don't know that for certain. That's my advice to you. It could be these complaints are unfounded. And there are laws in place to protect you against unruly neighbours."

"So, we just move to the cottage and take our chances?" Henry said.

"That's right."

"He's right, Henry," Rebecca said. "What else can we do? We're probably overreacting anyway. If the guests make too much noise, we can ask them to turn it down. People are generally reasonable."

"It looks like we don't have much choice, do we?" Henry said.

"I'd still like to know why Darren Needham is so against us going to the cottage at the weekend," Rebecca said. "Surely things can't be that bad."

"We'll soon find out. We'll be moving there for good soon."

"Why don't we go and see what the fuss is all about now?" It was Colin.

"I'm not following you," Henry said.

"It's still early," Colin said. "It's a beautiful day for a drive to the sea. We can make a day of it. There's no law that says we can't have a look at the cottage from the road."

"I don't know about that," Henry said. "It's a long drive."

"It's eighty-odd miles down the M3, dad. We can go in the people carrier. There's more than enough room for all of us. It'll do Katie and Paul good to get away from their tablets and phones for a while. We can get some sea air in our lungs. It's the school holidays so we won't have to rush back to get the twins ready for school tomorrow."

"Are you sure?" Rebecca asked.

"Dead sure. Give me an hour to round up the troops and I'll come back and pick you up. We can see for ourselves how bad Brightwater Lane is at the weekend."

"I'd better be off," Greg said and stood up. "Thanks for the tea."

"Thank you for seeing us on a Sunday," Henry said.

"I wouldn't worry too much. HomeFromHome has rules about disturbances too. They wouldn't risk their reputation on a few unruly guests."

"Thanks, Greg," Colin said.

"I'll see myself out."

Greg took out his mobile phone as soon as he got outside. He held it to his ear as he walked to his car. Henry watched him out of the window. He could see he was talking to someone on his phone but he couldn't hear what he was saying. Henry was unaware he was talking to Darren Needham. The legal practice Gregg Higgins worked for didn't only represent the accountancy company Colin was a part of – Gregg Higgins also did all of the conveyancing for Needham Properties.

## CHAPTER FOURTEEN

Even though the mood during the drive was upbeat Rebecca felt uneasy. Colin's Renault Grand Scenic was making short work of the distance to Frisk and they were over halfway there. Henry was sitting in the front with Colin – Rebecca and Susan were behind them and Katie and Paul occupied the fold-out seats right at the back. The twins hadn't spoken a word since they set off. Their eyes were glued to their mobile phones the whole time. Henry and Rebecca had decided not to take Alfred with them. The Jack Russell wasn't used to travelling long distances and they didn't want to traumatise him any more than necessary. He was used to spending long periods of time at home so they'd left him asleep on the sofa in the living room.

Rebecca wasn't sure what to expect. She didn't know what would be waiting for them when they got to Frisk. Would there be a welcoming committee of drunken louts – music blaring and screaming and shouting? For some reason Darren Needham had been adamant they stay away from Sea View Cottage on weekends. Why was he so keen to keep them away?

Henry turned around and looked at his wife. "Are you alright, love?"

Rebecca nodded. "Just a bit apprehensive."

"Me too."

"Everything will be alright," Susan said. "What's the worst that can happen?"

*We'll arrive to find a rave in full swing next door to the cottage,* Rebecca thought but kept her fears to herself.

"You need to be careful here," Henry told Colin as they ventured into the New Forest. "This is where we took a wrong turn and ended up on the way to Bournemouth."

"I've got the GPS on," Colin told him. "According to that we take a left just up ahead."

"There's a nice little pub in Frisk," Henry said. "The Frisk Arms. We can get some lunch there when we've had a look at the cottage."

"Sounds great," Susan said. "I can't wait to see the place."

She didn't have to wait long. Colin turned onto the coast road at Milford and soon they were on their way to Frisk. There were quite a few cars on the road and Colin had to drive carefully on the windy coast road.

Susan looked back at the twins. Katie and Paul were still glued to their phones.

"Put those things away. There's the sea over there. When was the last time you saw the sea?"

Katie looked out of the window, but Paul didn't even bother.

"I give up," Colin said. "We should have insisted the phones stayed at home."

"It's just up here," Henry said as they passed the Frisk Arms. "You go up this hill, turn right and the cottage is on the right-hand side of the road."

Colin reduced his speed as he drove past the houses on either side. Those on the right offered spectacular views of the Solent every now and then.

"There it is," Henry pointed to Sea View Cottage.

A white van was parked on the street outside the cottage next door and as they got closer Henry realised it was the same van that had been there the last time they were here. Colin parked behind it and Henry could now clearly see the writing on the side.

*Dawson's Cleaning Services – we clean up your mess so you don't have to.*

"Do you think the old owner has got someone in to clean the place before you move in?" Susan had seen the van too.

"They'll be here for next door," Henry guessed. "They were here last time too."

"Are you alright, mum?" Colin asked.

Rebecca had barely spoken a word since they set off.

She nodded. "The cottage looks different somehow."

"It looks exactly the same to me," Henry argued.

"Let's go and have a look, shall we?" Colin said and unclipped his seatbelt.

"Kids, this is where you'll be spending most of your summer holidays from now on."

"I love that garden," Susan said.

"You should see the view from the back," Henry said. "We're going to get up and look out onto the Isle of Wight every morning."

They all got out of the car and Henry stretched his arms out. Susan headed for the front gate. Colin walked towards the fence that separated Sea View Cottage from number 12. The blue of the Solent could be seen in the gap between the properties. Even the twins seemed to be taking a keen interest in the place.

"What do you think?" Rebecca asked.

"It's gorgeous," Susan said.

"It really is," Colin agreed.

He looked at the gate and tried the latch. "It's open. Shall we take a closer look?"

"We're not supposed to," Henry said.

"The cottage is all but yours," Susan said. "What harm can it do?"

"We're not going to break in," Colin added. "We can peek in the windows and get a closer look."

He opened the gate and walked up the path towards the house. Susan followed after him with the twins not far behind.

Henry reached down and took Rebecca's hand. "So far so good. I don't know why giraffe-neck was so keen to keep us away. It's as quiet as the grave here today."

"Perhaps we have been a bit paranoid," Rebecca looked up at the garden. "I didn't see those rhododendrons before. I love rhododendrons."

"I thought they were bad for the garden," Henry said.

"Not really. You just need to keep an eye on them."

The sound of a van door sliding open made Henry turn around. A man was throwing something into the van. It was the same man they'd seen when they were last here.

"I'm going to say hello," Henry said.

"I think I'll inspect the garden a bit more," Rebecca told him. "It looks like there's a lot I missed before."

Henry walked over to the white van. Another man had joined the first and neither of them looked too happy.

"Afternoon," Henry said to them. "Henry Green. Me and my wife have just bought the cottage next door."

The older of the two men nodded. "Good to meet you."

"Do you live here?"

"Not likely," the other man said. "We just get paid to clean up the shit."

"I'm not following you."

"The HomeFromHome," the older man explained. "We usually come and clean up on a Monday but we got a call earlier offering us Sunday rates so here we are. You don't turn down double-time. Are you going to be living here?"

"Why else would we have bought the place?" Henry asked.

"HomeFromHome," the younger man said. "The town is full of 'em. Easy way to make some extra money."

"If you've got someone like Dawson's Cleaning to get rid of the carnage after the guests clear off," his colleague said. "We'd better get back to work – this latest lot were a bunch of animals. Left the place in a right state."

The two men walked back through the gate of number 12 without saying anything further.

Henry found his family in the back garden. There was a path that ran along the side of the cottage.

"This is lovely, dad," Colin said.

"I don't think I'd ever get tired of that view," Susan added.

Even the twins seemed to be content without their phones and tablets in their hands. Katie and Paul were inspecting something at the end of the garden.

"Who were those men in the van?" Rebecca asked.

"Some cleaning company," Henry said and didn't elaborate further.

Rebecca looked much more relaxed now and Henry didn't want to ruin that with his fears about what they were getting themselves into.

*What had the older cleaning man said?* He thought. *Bunch of animals – left the place in a right state.*

What exactly *were* they getting themselves into?

## CHAPTER FIFTEEN

After a nice lunch at the Frisk Arms Colin decided he wanted to have another look at Sea View Cottage before they made their way back to London. It was just after three in the afternoon, and he just wanted to take a quick look before they set off back. The three pints of local ale Henry had polished off at the pub hadn't done anything to quell the unease he'd felt after his conversation with the men from the cleaning company. If Dawson's Cleaning came to the cottage next door on a regular basis, what exactly did that mean? Were the guests who rented out number 12 really that bad?

"There's someone next door," Rebecca said.

"It's probably the men I spoke to," Henry said.

"On the other side," Rebecca said. "In the garden of number 8."

Henry looked out of the car window. An old woman was watering some pot plants next to the front door. Henry thought she looked to be at least seventy. Her hair was long, but it was completely grey. She was wearing a floral dress and she was very thin.

"Shall we go and say hello?" Rebecca said. "She could be our new next-door-neighbour."

"Well, she doesn't look like a HomeFromHome guest," Henry said. "What harm can it do?"

Colin parked the car and Henry and Rebecca got out.

"Aren't you coming?" Rebecca asked.

"We don't want to scare the old duck," Colin said. "We'll leave you in peace to get to know your new neighbour."

Henry stood by the gate to number 8. "Hello there."

The elderly woman didn't even look up. She filled up a watering can from a tap in the garden and walked back towards her pot plants."

"Hello!" Henry shouted again, louder this time.

The old lady carried on watering her plants.
"Perhaps she's a bit deaf," Rebecca suggested.
"Or just plain rude," Henry said. "I'm beginning to think that a prerequisite to living in Frisk is to pass some kind of rudeness test first."
"Don't be silly. Maybe she just doesn't want to be disturbed."

The old lady had spotted them and what she did next surprised Henry and Rebecca. She waved then smiled at them. She put down her watering can and went inside the house. She came out a short while later and walked over to the gate.
"Sorry about that." Her accent wasn't local.
Henry thought he detected a hint of American in there.
"I don't put in my aids unless I have to," she added.
"Aids?" Henry said.
She tapped her ear.
"Ah," Rebecca said. "Hearing aids."
"It's almost gone now. My hearing, I mean. I can still sense vibrations and very loud noises but without the aids, I'm as deaf as a post."
"We've just bought the cottage next door," Henry told her. "Henry and Rebecca Green."
"Sea View Cottage is beautiful. Lily and Peter really looked after the place. My name is Mary. Mary Major. Pleased to meet you."
She held out a very pale hand. Henry and Rebecca both shook it.

"We brought some of the family down to have a look at the place," Henry told her.
"Would you like to come in for a cup of tea?" Mary asked and turned to Henry and sniffed the air. "Or perhaps something stronger? I see you're a man who likes a drink."
"I had a few pints of the local brew at the pub," Henry said.

"That's the thing about losing one of your senses," Mary said. "You tend to overcompensate with the other four. I have the sense of smell of a bloodhound. I've got some beer in the fridge. It's American but it's bearable if you take a deep breath before you drink it."

"We've got the kids and grandkids in the car," Rebecca said. "Maybe next time."

"We'll be moving here for good in the next few weeks," Henry said.

"Then I shall look forward to it."

Colin and Susan appeared behind them.

"This is our son and daughter-in-law," Rebecca said.

"Where are the twins?" Henry asked Colin.

"Where do you think?" Colin said. "Attached to their phones."

"This is Mrs Major," Rebecca said.

"Call me Mary," she insisted. "Are you sure you won't come in for a quick drink?"

"Do you need to get back?" Rebecca asked Colin.

"It's still pretty early," Colin said. "The roads should be quiet on the way back so I don't think a quick drink will hurt."

"Will the twins be alright on their own?" Henry asked.

"They won't even notice we've gone," Susan said.

Mary led them inside the cottage and the first thing Henry realised was it was almost identical to Sea View Cottage. The layout was the same and the rooms seemed to be the same size. It was clear that whoever had built the properties on Brightwater Lane had built them to the same specifications. Bookshelves lined every wall in the living room and on closer inspection Henry realised Mary was a fan of crime fiction. All genres of murder mysteries filled the shelves. From psychological thrillers to cosy mystery, it was clear Mary liked to read them all. On a sideboard in the corner stood some framed black-and-white photographs. A much younger Mary Major was in some of them as was a very tall man in an army uniform.

"That's the colonel," Mary told him.

"Colonel?" Colin said. "Impressive."

"My William. He's been gone for nearly twenty years now. He loved it here."

"And you stayed here by yourself?" Rebecca asked.

"Where else would I go? Shall we sit outside?"

She led them out into the back garden. "I'll fix us some drinks."

"She seems nice," Susan said when Mary was busy with the drinks.

"I'm starting to wonder if we've been worrying about nothing," Rebecca said.

"I think you're right, love," Henry said. "So what if there's a HomeFromHome next door – we've got an old lady on the other side, and I very much doubt the colonel's wife is going to make too much noise."

"You're going to have a wonderful life here," Susan said. "A really wonderful life."

## CHAPTER SIXTEEN

The afternoon sun was far behind Mary Major's house. Henry, Rebecca, Colin and Susan were still sitting outside in the garden. Susan had just come back from checking on the twins.

"I told you," she said. "They didn't even realise we'd gone."

"You're American, aren't you?" Henry said.

"The colonel and I came here fifty years ago," Mary replied. "But the accent is impossible to hide. William was stationed not far from here during the war and he fell in love with the place. Of course, he wasn't a colonel during the war. That came later."

"And you've been in Frisk for all that time?" Colin asked.

"Oh no. We were in Southampton. We bought the cottage just before William passed. The colonel was quite a bit older than me."

"Do you have children?" Rebecca said. "Grandchildren?"

"Unfortunately, not. The colonel was enough for me."

"I don't think I've ever met a colonel," Henry said and finished what was left in the bottle of beer.

"He was an amazing man," Mary said. "He was nineteen when the Second World War broke out and he saw some horrendous things. He was one of the first to arrive in Pearl Harbour. He was posted over here right before the end of it all."

"Wow," Colin said.

"Then a few years later he was called to Korea," Mary continued.

"And Vietnam I suppose?" Henry asked.

"He was lucky enough to have risen up the ranks before that debacle. He didn't see much action in Vietnam. Do you know he went straight from Captain to Lieutenant Colonel?"

"I'm not too clued up about army ranks," Colin admitted.

"He skipped Major," Henry educated him.

"Major Major," Mary said and started to laugh. "I suppose his commanding officers didn't have much of a sense of humour. Anyway, he retired as a colonel and that's pretty much it."

"I very much doubt that," Henry said. "What a fascinating life you must have led."

"We've been blessed with a good life."

"What's it like living here?" Henry said. "With all the holiday rentals in the village, I mean?"

"It doesn't bother me at all."

"What about the noise they make?" Rebecca said. "I believe there have been some complaints about all the noise."

Mary tapped her ear again. "If there is any noise, I switch the aids off. Sometimes deafness is a blessing."

Henry didn't doubt it. But, unfortunately there was nothing wrong with his ears.

"Did you know the previous owners of Sea View Cottage well?" he asked. "I apologise if I seem a bit too inquisitive."

"Henry used to be a schoolteacher," Rebecca explained.

"I thought so," Mary said. "Lily passed away last year and her husband, Peter joined her a couple of months ago."

"I'm sorry to hear about that," Rebecca said.

"We really should get going," Susan said. "It's getting late and Colin has a management meeting first thing in the morning."

"Thanks for reminding me," Colin said.

"Thank you for the drinks, Mary," Henry said. "It's been really nice getting to know you."

"Likewise," Mary said. "It's been nice to enjoy some company for a change. The colonel was the sociable one, you see – I don't get out much anymore."

The twins were fast asleep when they returned to the car. Katie and Paul were both slumped forwards in the back. Both of them still held their mobile phones in their hands.

Susan yawned. "What a wonderful afternoon."

"Wasn't it just," Colin agreed. "Mrs Major seemed like quite a character. I bet she's got a whole load of stories to tell."

"And she likes her gardening," Rebecca added.

"And her books," Henry chipped in. "I've got a feeling we're going to enjoy living next door to the colonel's wife."

The first part of the trip home passed by in silence. Rebecca and Susan had nodded off and Henry was finding it hard not to do the same. The three pints at the Frisk Arms and the two bottles of Becks had made him very sleepy but he wanted to stay awake to keep his son company.

They'd just passed Winchester when Henry finally succumbed. His head fell forward, his breathing became heavier and very soon he was snoring loudly on the passenger seat. Colin looked at him and smiled. All in all, it had been a really great day, and the reservations they'd all had about the move to Frisk had been dispelled somewhat.

Henry woke when they were just on the outskirts of London. He looked out of the window and saw the murk of the Thames as they crossed the bridge at Kingston.

"Sorry about dropping off, son," he said to Colin.

Colin gave a backward nod of his head. "You weren't the only one, dad."

"I think the sea air knocked us all out."

"It's supposed to have that effect on people," Colin agreed. "Although it might have been the beer you knocked back. Almost home."

Colin stopped outside his parents' house and turned off the engine.

"Do you want to come in for some tea?" Henry asked him.

"We'd better be off," Colin said. "I'd totally forgotten about the meeting tomorrow and there are a few things I need to go through this evening."

"Thanks for today, son? Your mother and me really appreciate what you've done. It really helped to put our minds at ease."

"No problem, dad. Are you going to start moving things in next week?"

"I'm not sure. It's a bit of a trek to keep going back and forth – I think I'd prefer to get it over and done with in one go. I'll phone some removal companies tomorrow. I suppose we should wake your mother up."

# CHAPTER SEVENTEEN

The big day arrived two weeks later. Easter had come and gone – the school holidays were over and Henry and Rebecca Green were ready for the move to Frisk. Darren Needham had informed them the funds had been transferred from the sale of the house in Wimbledon and Sea Cottage was officially theirs. They'd also been told the balance owing to them after the legal fees and commission was just under a hundred-thousand-pounds. According to the lanky estate agent this money would be in their account before the end of the week.

Henry and Rebecca had spent the two weeks tying up loose ends and saying their goodbyes. Henry had been quite surprised at how easy it had been bidding farewell to a huge chunk of his and Rebecca's lives. Wimbledon looked different to them now – their home for more than forty years seemed grimier and dingier than it had when they'd been a part of the woodwork there and they were looking forward to their new lives in Frisk with an optimism they hadn't felt in years.

"All set?" Henry asked Rebecca outside a house that was no longer theirs.

"I'm ready if you are," Rebecca told him.

The removal company were already on their way to Frisk and Henry and Rebecca had stayed behind to do a last-minute check of the house. Now, after making sure they hadn't left anything behind they were ready to set off. Alfred was already in the car. Henry had placed his favourite blanket on the back seat and the Jack Russell was now fast asleep. Darren Needham had arranged to meet them at Sea View Cottage to hand over the keys. Colin and Phoebe had both taken a couple of days off work and were due to meet them at the new cottage in a couple of hours to help them get unpacked.

Henry realised he had a spring in his step as he and Rebecca walked to the car. This was a new beginning, and he was more excited than he'd been in years. He had a sudden urge to take Rebecca in his arms and dance with her to where he'd parked the car. He managed to control himself – Henry was a reserved man and that would be taking things a bit too far.

He couldn't resist opening the passenger door for Rebecca though.

"After you, Mrs Green."

Rebecca beamed at him. "Why thank you, Mr Green."

* * *

They arrived in Frisk just under two hours later. Colin's Renault was already parked outside, and Henry and Rebecca's son was talking to one of the removal men. Henry and Rebecca walked over to them. Alfred had slept all the way there and now he was tugging on his lead.

"You got here quick," Rebecca said.

"I set off a bit earlier," Colin told her. "Darren Needham gave me the keys when I got here so we could make a start. I hope you don't mind."

"Of course not," Henry said.

"Where's Mr Needham now?" Rebecca asked.

"He had to leave. He asked me to pass on his apologies."

"I'm glad he's not here," Henry said. "He's earned his piece of the pie, so good riddance to him."

"It looks like that little fella wants to explore the garden," Colin pointed to Alfred.

The Jack Russell was tugging even harder at his lead.

"Come on then, Alfie," Henry said. "Let's see how you like your new house."

"The removal men seem very professional," Colin said to Rebecca.

"They're going to take the big things in first then finish off with the boxes."

"They're all labelled," Rebecca said. "You know what I'm like."

It had taken her quite a while to work through her list. Colin and Susan now had a garage full of stuff they'd chosen – a number of charity shops in Wimbledon were considerably better stocked and the rest of Henry and Rebecca's things had been thrown away. Rebecca was confident they'd only brought the things they would need at Sea View Cottage.

One of the removal men approached. He was a plump man in his mid-forties.

"Sorry to bother you," he said. "But we might have a problem with the three-seater. Looks like the door's too narrow to get it in."

Rebecca sighed. They'd had the leather sofa for years. She was sure it was still the same one they'd had when Colin and Phoebe still lived at home.

"We can try and shove it through," the removal man added. "But it looks like it'll be a tight squeeze."

"If you could," Rebecca said. "If not we'll have to get something smaller."

"I'll take some measurements. And old Bob there has a few tricks up his sleeve. He once managed to get a baby grand piano up a fire escape, you know."

After numerous attempts and much puffing and panting it was clear the old three-seater wasn't going to fit. No matter which way the removal men tried turning it the leather sofa wouldn't fit through the doorframe.

"What now?" Henry asked Rebecca.

"We'll have to buy a new one," she said. "A smaller one."

"I liked that sofa."

"It was past its best anyway. And we can afford a nice new one with the money left over from the old house. It'll be a new sofa for a new house. A new beginning all round."

They managed to get everything else they'd brought with them from London inside the cottage. Phoebe had arrived and now she and Rebecca were unpacking boxes in the kitchen. Henry and Colin were setting up the television and the surround-sound in the living room. The room looked very empty without the three-seater sofa. The only other chairs they had were Henry's old armchair and an oak chair they used to use in the bedroom back in Wimbledon.

"Where are the remotes?" Colin asked. "All the cables and speakers are here but I can't find the remote controls."

"They're in the boot of the car," Henry remembered. "I didn't want them to go missing during the move. I'll go and get them."

Phoebe was outside in the front garden when Henry came out.

"This is lovely, dad," she said. "You and mum are going to be very happy here."

"I think so too, love," Henry said. "I left the remotes for the television and the home theatre in the car."

He was halfway to his car when a very short, red-faced man stopped him.

"Hello," Henry said.

"Are you the new owners?" the man asked.

"We've just bought the place."

"The name's King," the man didn't offer his hand. "Lionel King. Me and the wife live across the road. Are you planning on living here?"

"Of course."

"Good luck with that."

"What's that supposed to mean?" Henry said.

"You'll see. You know what happened to the previous owners, do you?"

"I believe they passed away."

"Murdered, more like it."

Phoebe came over to them. She couldn't help hearing what Mr King was saying.

"What's going on?"

"I really have no idea, love," Henry said.

"Those bastards in the HomeFromHome rentals might as well have put a gun to their heads and pulled the trigger," Lionel continued. "My Diana is going the same way. Nerves are shot. That's what happened to Lily and Peter – their nerves couldn't take it anymore."

"I really have no idea what you're talking about," Henry said. "We've got a lot of unpacking still to do, so you won't mind if we get on."

"You'll see," Lionel wasn't giving up. "You'll see when they descend on us in their droves. Weekends are the worst, but we get some who stay all week. I tried to get lawyers involved but all that costs money and my pension isn't what it used to be. And there's not many of us left – we're outnumbered, you see. The HomeFromHome places are taking over. And the colonel's wife doesn't seem to notice, what with her ears and all."

"Have you quite finished?" Phoebe asked.

"Do yourselves a favour." It was clear he wasn't. "Get out. Get out now, before you go the same way as the previous owners of Sea View Cottage."

## CHAPTER EIGHTEEN

"What an angry old man," Phoebe said when Lionel King had marched back across the road. "I'd steer well clear of him if I were you."

"He seemed quite sure about these HomeFromHome rentals," Henry said. "And he's not the first to voice concerns."

"That man is just naturally angry. I've seen his sort before. He's the kind of man who phones the police when a neighbour's dog barks in the night. I wouldn't worry about Lionel King. Let's get back to work, shall we?"

It was starting to get dark by the time they were done for the day. They were nowhere near finished but all of them were dog-tired and Rebecca had decided they'd done enough to make Sea View Cottage habitable.

"Let's grab a bite to eat at the Frisk Arms," Henry suggested.

"Sounds like a plan," Colin agreed.

"I hadn't given much thought to what we were going to eat," Rebecca said.

"We can get something to eat without having to worry about cooking," Henry said. "Colin and Phoebe are staying the night anyway, so they don't have to drive back to London."

"And you get to sample some more of that local ale?" Colin added.

"That too," Henry said. "Our treat. It can be a thank you for all your help."

Rebecca insisted on having a bath before they left for the pub. Henry, Colin and Phoebe were taking a well-earned break on the patio in the back garden. Henry had brought some beers with him, and they were all enjoying the early evening warmth.

"Did dad tell you about the angry pixie from across the road?" Phoebe asked Colin.

"No," Colin said.

"Lionel the Loony," Phoebe said. "He marched across the road and did his best to scare us."

"That doesn't sound good," Colin said.

"He was one beer short of a sixpack," Henry said. "I won't be speaking to him again in a hurry if I can help it."

"What did he say?" Colin asked.

"All kinds of stuff about these HomeFromHome places," Phoebe said. "He as good as told dad to get out while he still could."

"Did you tell mum?"

"No," Henry said. "And I'm not planning on telling her. Your mother doesn't need to worry about angry neighbours. I'm starving. We should get going."

They decided to walk to the Frisk Arms. It was a beautiful late-April evening and the walk there was all downhill. Colin pointed out that it would be an uphill climb on the way back, but Henry argued they wouldn't notice if they drank enough local beer.

The pub was relatively quiet, and Henry was glad. He hadn't realised how hungry he was – they'd been too preoccupied with the unpacking to even think about food. They sat at a table by the window and Henry and Colin went to the bar to get some drinks.

The same man and woman were working behind the bar as before – a middle-aged couple with very friendly faces. One of the man's eyes looked like it was made from glass – it stared directly ahead the whole time, unblinking.

"What can I get you?" he asked.

"A couple of pints of the Cat's Whiskers," Henry replied. "And two glasses of red wine please. Are you doing food?"

The man pointed to a board behind the bar. "Those are the specials for this evening. I'll bring the drinks over."

Henry thanked him and he and Colin returned to the table.

"The specials are on the board," Henry said. "I quite like the look of the gammon."

"I think I'll have the same," Rebecca said.

"This place is lovely," Phoebe said. "Very quaint. There aren't many pubs like this left."

"This is going to be our new local," Henry said. "I could get used to that Cat's Whiskers."

The barman arrived with the drinks and put them on the table.

"Are you here on holiday?"

"We've just moved here," Rebecca told him.

An eyebrow was raised above the barman's good eye. "You moved to Frisk?"

"We bought Sea View Cottage," Henry said.

"Lily and Peter's place?"

"So I believe. Did you know them?"

"They popped in here from time to time. Quiet people."

"What happened to them?" Phoebe asked. "We had the pleasure of meeting Mr King from across the road and he said they both passed away, but he was very vague. He seemed like he wasn't all there to me."

The barman smiled. "You're not wrong there. Lionel is alright, but he has a habit of rubbing people up the wrong way. I'm Dave, by the way. Me and my wife, Penny run this place."

"Henry Green," Henry told him. "This is my wife, Rebecca, and our kids, Colin and Phoebe."

"Mr King mentioned something about the HomeFromHome guests making a nuisance of themselves," Phoebe said.

Henry looked at her and gave a subtle shake of the head.

"I've heard they can sometimes be a problem," Dave said.

"I suppose you get a lot of them in here," Henry said.

"Not as many as you'd think. We used to when the families rented the HomeFromHome places, but things have changed a bit of late."

"What do you mean?" Rebecca said.

"Let's just say in recent times the calibre of guests has changed. They don't seem to come here for the same reasons anymore. They bring their own booze and food and rarely venture out. Frisk is a beautiful part of the country. We've got the National Park on our doorstep and the sea a stone's-throw away but all these new types of guests seem to want to do is drink the day and night away. It doesn't make any sense to me – surely they can do that at home. I'd better get on. Have you decided what you want to eat?"

"I think we're all going to have the gammon," Henry looked around the table.

The nods from Rebecca, Colin and Phoebe confirmed this.

"Four gammons it is then," Dave said and walked back to the bar.

"What do you think he meant by that?" Rebecca said. "About the guests not even leaving the HomeFromHome rentals?"

"I don't think it's that bad, mum," Colin said. "How would he even know? Just because they don't come to the pub, doesn't mean they don't leave the houses."

"Colin's right," Phoebe said. "Who in their right mind would pay to rent out a property in such a lovely part of the country and not even venture out to see what's on offer?"

"I suppose you're right," Rebecca said.

"I hope that gammon doesn't take long," Henry said. "I'm starving."

This wasn't true. In fact, Henry's appetite had gone. Something was stirring in the pit of his stomach, and it wasn't hunger pains. Everybody they had spoken to in the short time they'd arrived in Frisk had the same story to tell about the HomeFromHome rentals and Henry was starting to realise their move to Sea View Cottage had been a terrible mistake.

## CHAPTER NINETEEN

They got their first taste of *the guests* four days later. It was Friday afternoon, and the May Day long weekend was upon them. Henry and Rebecca had settled nicely into Sea View Cottage. Everything was unpacked and the cottage was starting to feel like home. Colin, Susan and the twins were due to arrive the next day and the weather forecast looked promising. Rebecca had made all kind of plans for the long weekend. A trip to the sea was a must – they'd been in the cottage for almost a week now and they'd been so preoccupied with getting the place in order, they hadn't even made the short trip to the sea they could see from the back garden.

Henry looked up from his newspaper. "Looks like it's going to be a nice bank holiday for a change. The forecast looks good."

"I can't wait to take the twins to the sea," Rebecca said. "We can get fish and chips and sit on the beach."

"Sounds lovely."

"What do you feel like for tea?" Rebecca asked.

"How about one of those pies you made earlier in the week?"

"I'll take a couple out the freezer. They ought to defrost quickly in this weather."

Henry turned his head and frowned. "What's that noise?"

"Music." Rebecca had heard it too.

The music was loud and it was accompanied by the sound of voices. A car door slammed, and the music stopped.

"That's odd," Henry said.

He got up from his chair and walked over to the window.

"Is someone next door?" Rebecca asked.

"Two cars. Fancy ones by the looks of things. There's a whole load of people walking up the path – six or seven of them. I don't know where they're all going to sleep. I thought there was a limit to how many guests they could accommodate."

"They rent out the whole property," Rebecca said. "Whether it's one guest or ten, it's the same price."

"There should be a law against that many people staying."

It didn't stop at seven. Over the course of the next two hours, more cars arrived. Two shiny 4x4s and a convertible BMW were now parked in the road opposite the cottage. All of them had announced their arrival with a fanfare of loud music. Henry stood sentry by the window at the front.

"That's fifteen people," he told Rebecca. "Surely that's not allowed."

"Perhaps only a few of them are actually staying the night," Rebecca suggested. "There is no way there's enough room for fifteen people in there."

The music started soon afterwards. It wasn't exactly offensive - it was something from the 1980s, but it was extremely loud.

"I hope that's not going to carry on all night," Rebecca said.

"It could be worse," Henry said. "They could be playing that awful hip-hop stuff our Phoebe got into for a while."

"Well, it's too loud. I'm going to make a start on tea. The pies should be defrosted by now."

Henry picked up his book and went outside to the back garden. The music was louder out here, and it soon became clear the speakers had been placed outside. A group of men and women in their mid-forties were standing in the garden with drinks in their hands. One of them, a tall man with balding, brown hair spotted Henry and waved. Henry didn't wave back. He turned his attention back to his book. The tall man didn't get the hint.

"Alright." He was now standing next to the fence.

Henry looked up and saw he was holding a can of Stella in his hand.

"Alright," he said once more.

Henry nodded at him.

"Things might get a bit rowdy this weekend," the man informed him.

The music seemed even louder now.

Henry sighed, put down his book and walked over to the fence.

"We're having a reunion," the man said and took a huge swig from the can.

"Class of 89. Like I say things might get a bit out of hand a bit later."

Henry couldn't believe what he was hearing. "Would it be possible to keep the noise down a bit?"

The man started to laugh. "I can ask them, but I wouldn't get your hopes up. Some of us haven't seen each other for twenty-odd years and we've got a lot of catching up to do – you know what it's like."

"Could you please do your reminiscing at a lower volume, then?"

"You're funny, mate."

A woman with short blond hair joined him by the fence. "Who's your new friend, Si?"

She was clearly already drunk.

"Local," the man called Si told her. "He's asking if we can keep the noise down."

"Not bloody likely," she said. "Sorry, mate."

"This is a residential area," Henry informed her. "There are rules about noise."

"After midnight it says on the HomeFromHome website. Quiet time after 12pm it says."

Henry looked at his watch. It was now almost five in the afternoon.

"Quiet time after 12pm?" he said.

"That's what it says," the woman said and laughed. "Rules are rules."

"You can't argue with that," Si agreed.

"I've asked you nicely to please turn it down a bit," Henry said. "My wife and I live here and we came here for some peace and quiet."

"We're on holiday," the woman said. "We've paid for the weekend and we're going to bloody well enjoy ourselves. If it makes you feel any better, we'll turn it down after 12pm like it says on the website."

Henry could see it was pointless arguing. But this didn't prevent him from educating the drunk woman about ante-meridiem and post-meridiem. "If you are adamant about adhering strictly to the HomeFromHome rules," he said. "I would be very grateful. It's a common mistake people make but 12pm is in fact midday. Midnight is the starting point of the new day and therefore it cannot be the post-meridiem of a day to which it does not belong."

"What?" the woman said and opened her mouth wide.

"I think he's trying to fool us, Sam," Si said.

"I'm trying to educate you. The teachers from the class of '89 clearly did a rather inadequate job."

## CHAPTER TWENTY

Henry's lesson on PM and AM clearly had little effect on the reunion guests next door. It was now almost nine and the noise from next door was even worse.

"Perhaps we should phone the police," Rebecca suggested.

"I don't think there's a police station here in Frisk," Henry said.

"Surely this kind of racket is against the law."

"We don't even have the number of the nearest police station," Henry said. "It's probably in Milford."

"I'm going to look it up. I'm not putting up with this all night."

She found a number for the police in Milford and saved it to her phone. The noise next door had reached an unbearable level. The music had been turned up and it was now accompanied by the voices of people who were clearly intoxicated. One woman in particular had a cackle that Henry found extremely offensive. Every now and then her hacking laugh could be heard over the cacophony and Henry would find himself wincing. Rebecca was starting to get a headache.

After a few unsuccessful attempts she was finally put through to someone on call in Milford. What she was told wasn't what she was hoping to hear. After explaining the situation three times she was informed it wasn't possible to send someone out. All the police officers were otherwise engaged and a concern about noise levels was, in fact a matter for the council and not the police.

"I cannot believe this," Rebecca said to Henry when she'd ended the call. "They said there's nothing they can do."

Someone next door screamed so loud Henry's eyes opened wide when he heard it.

"You're so fucking funny, Si!"

"Surely that is against the law," he said. "Shouting the F word like that in public has to be against the law."

"The man I spoke to said it's a council matter," Rebecca told him. "The police won't come out for nuisance neighbours anymore."

"That's ridiculous. What *will* it take for them to come out? When one of those hooligans next door attacks us?"

"He suggested we try and talk to them," Rebecca said. "And failing that we can contact the council to try and stop it from happening again."

"How long is that going to take? It's not going to get them to turn the damn noise down tonight, is it?"

"We could try and talk to them again. Ask them to tone it down a bit."

"They're blotto," Henry reminded her. "You cannot reason with a drunk person – I already tried and I got nowhere."

"I'll have a go," Rebecca said. "You can come across a bit confusing sometimes with the way you say things."

"I speak English. It's not my fault nobody seems to understand their own language these days."

Henry insisted on going with Rebecca. The guests next door had been knocking back the booze for hours now and he wasn't going to let his wife talk to them without backup. The music playing was shaking the windows in Sea View Cottage. All the guests were outside now. Some of them were dancing and others were trying to talk over the booming music blasting out of the speakers. A woman was being sick in the rose bushes at the end of the garden.

"That's just disgusting," Rebecca said. "They're grown adults – how can they behave like this?"

They walked up to the fence.

"Hello!" Rebecca shouted.

It was useless. The din next door was far too loud.

Henry put two fingers in his mouth and let rip with such a deafening whistle Rebecca had to cover her ears. It seemed to do the trick. A few of the reunion guests turned and looked in their direction.

"That never fails," Henry said to Rebecca. "It's something I learned when I was teaching."

Four men and a woman staggered up to the fence. One of them – a man wearing glasses almost fell over as he walked.

"Could you please turn it down?" Rebecca asked.

"What?" the woman bellowed.

Henry tried to tell them what they wanted with gestures. He put the fingers of both hands together and waved them downwards a few times. It didn't work.

"Do you want to join us?" the woman screamed.

"No," Rebecca screamed back. "We don't want to join you. We're asking you to keep the noise down. It's gone ten and it's time to turn it down."

"Do you want a drink?" the man in the glasses took a can of beer from a four-pack and held it out.

"Come and join us," the woman said. "We're pissed."

"We just want a bit of peace," Henry said. "Surely it's against the HomeFromHome rules to have so many people in one house."

"We've booked three HomeFromHomes," the woman said.

"Numbers 12, 14 and 16," a chubby man elaborated. "Not that it's any of your bloody business."

The man wearing the glasses lurched to the side and was caught just in time by the chubby man. Two of the beers he was holding fell to the ground – one of them burst open and spun round and round, releasing a spray of foam as it spun. Henry was hit in the face by the spray and took a step backwards. The woman turned around and walked back towards the cottage.

Soon afterwards the music was turned down a notch. The damaged beer can was spinning more slowly now.

Henry approached the fence again and wiped his face. "Keep the noise down. Keep it down or we're calling the police."

The chubby man started to laugh. "Go for it."

"Excuse me," Rebecca said.

"We're not doing any harm," he told her. "We're trying to enjoy the reunion and all we're getting is grief about nothing."

"You are disturbing the peace," Henry said. "You're making too much noise."

"You've just forgotten how to enjoy yourself." Another man said.

"The music's been turned down," the chubby man said. "What's your fucking problem?"

Henry was about to reply when he felt Rebecca's hand on his shoulder. She nodded to him, and they both went back inside their cottage.

"You can't reason with them in that state," she said in the kitchen.

Henry turned on the kettle. "What do we do, then? The police aren't interested – the council will probably do sod all, so what do you suggest we do about it?"

"I don't know, love," Rebecca said. "I really don't know."

But as she sat in the living room sipping her tea listening to the din coming from the guests next door she could feel her face heating up. Her heartbeat was racing, and her blood felt like it was boiling. As she sat there with her tea, she felt utterly helpless and it was a feeling she didn't like. She couldn't remember the last time she'd felt so furious. The sound of a bottle breaking could be heard next door and Rebecca knew they had to do something. She wasn't quite sure how she was going to do it, but she was going to do something to stop the HomeFromHome rentals from ruining their dream retirement.

"The noise has stopped," Henry stated the obvious just after midnight.

This wasn't quite true. The music had been switched off but the sound of voices could still be heard. Car doors were slammed and then the voices were outside on the road at the front. Soon afterwards the silence was so absolute it felt unnaturally quiet somehow.

"Thank God for that," Henry said. "I'm off to bed."

"Me too," Rebecca said.

"Let's hope they've got it out of their systems," Henry added. "They won't be able to do that two nights in a row. They'll probably be quiet tomorrow."

"Probably," Rebecca said.

"It's a shame there seems to be nothing we can do about it."

"No," Rebecca said.

*Nothing according to the law*, she kept this thought unspoken.

## CHAPTER TWENTY ONE

Colin, Susan and the twins arrived early the next morning. The class of '89 reunion guests hadn't yet surfaced next door and Rebecca wondered if the rowdy behaviour from the precious night was a one-off. Surely they wouldn't be up to putting in a repeat performance so soon.

"Wow," Colin exclaimed when he went inside the cottage. "I can't believe what you've done to the place in less than a week."

"It's like you've been here most of your lives," Susan added.

The twins stood in the living room. Katie and Paul seemed unsure what to do. Both of them shifted from side to side in the unfamiliar surroundings. For as long as they could remember they'd spent the majority of their time with their grandparents upstairs playing on the computer, but here at Sea View Cottage there was no upstairs, and they weren't even sure the computer had been set up yet.

"Don't even think about it." Susan knew the twins too well by now. "We're not here to spend hours inside playing games – the weather is lovely and we're going to do things as a family. I told you – no phones, tablets and definitely no computer. Go and play outside."

"They'll get used to it in no time." Henry had come inside the room. "Does anyone want some tea?"

"I'll make it," Susan offered. "We were just telling Rebecca how much you've done in such a short time. It's like you've brought the old house here and planted it in this very spot."

"We had to chuck a few things out," Rebecca said. "But it's surprising how much of our stuff could fit inside the cottage."

"That's new," Susan pointed to the green leather three-piece-suite.

"The old one wouldn't fit through the door," Henry said. "Shall we go outside to the garden?"

Before they'd even reached the door to the kitchen the twins came running back inside. Katie looked like she'd seen a ghost.

"What's wrong, love?" Rebecca asked her.

The nine-year-old girl didn't reply. She stood with her mouth open. Paul's eyes were wide and he kept looking behind him.

"What is it?" Susan said.

"Katie?" Colin joined in. "Paul?"

"There's a man and a woman," Katie found her voice at last.

"Next door?" Rebecca said. "It'll be some of the HomeFromHome lot. They're having a reunion and they made a bit of a nuisance of themselves last night. We had to ask them to keep it down."

"They were doing things," Paul told them.

"Doing things?" Susan repeated.

"Rude things," Katie elaborated.

Susan was out of the room in seconds. Colin, Rebecca and Henry followed her out to the back garden. The sound of a woman giggling could be heard from next door.

"Someone will see us," the woman said and giggled again.

"Someone already *has* seen you." It was Susan.

At the bottom of the garden next door a man and a woman who looked to be in their late-forties emerged from behind a high hedge and started to laugh. The man was bare-chested and the woman's bra was in danger of falling off. Both of them were very red in the face.

"What the hell do you think you're doing?" Susan shouted.

"What do you think?" the man replied.

"There are children here," Colin said. "Nine-year-old children."

"Well, they shouldn't be looking," the woman said.

"No," Henry joined in. "You shouldn't be out frolicking half-naked where anyone can see you."

"The kids didn't have to look," the man clearly wasn't finished yet.

That was it. Susan walked over to the fence.

"If you do not put your clothes back on right this instant I'm jumping over that fence and so help me God, I won't be responsible for what happens."

The man raised both hands in the air. "Alright. Chill. We didn't mean any harm – we were just having a bit of fun."

"We're on holiday," the woman added.

Some people had come outside of number 12 to see what the commotion was. Henry recognised the chubby man from the night before. He looked as sick as a dog. His hair was unbrushed and his grey pallor and bloodshot eyes suggested he'd had far too much to drink last night.

"What's going on, Liz?" he asked the still half-naked woman.

"The neighbours are complaining again," she said.

"What have we done now?"

"My kids came outside and were greeted with pornography," Susan said. "That's what. They're nine-years-old."

"It's probably nothing they ain't seen before," the woman called Liz said. She'd managed to straighten her bra and put on her blouse.

"It's disgusting," Henry said.

"Alright," the chubby man said. "Calm down, mate."

He rubbed his eyes. "I need something greasy inside me. My stomach feels like it hates me, and my head is throbbing."

"There's a pub down the road," Liz said. "We can probably get some breakfast there."

"Sounds like a plan," the chubby man said. "The rest of the gang won't be arriving for another few hours anyway."

"Rest of the gang?" Henry said. "You mean there are more people coming?"

"Too right, mate. Last night was just the dress rehearsal – the real party is taking place tonight."

"Just keep the noise down," Rebecca said. "We do not want a repeat of last night. We've got the grandkids here."

"We've paid for three cottages and we're going to get our money's worth."

Henry thought about this. He realised it was pointless arguing with this obnoxious man but perhaps he would listen to reason.

"Why do you have to have the reunion right next door to us? Why can't you have your party at number 14 or 16?"

"Number twelve has the best view," the chubby man replied.

"Best view?" Colin joined in. "What do you care about the view? You're here to piss it up – what difference does the view make?"

"Are you starting something with me, pal?"

"Don't tempt me."

"You're lucky I've got a thick head, mate. You're fucking lucky I don't jump over that fence right now."

Susan placed her hand on her husband's shoulder. "Come on. Let's go back inside. There's no point in trying to reason with people like this."

"You need to watch your fucking mouth, pal," the chubby man said.

# CHAPTER TWENTY TWO

"They can't get away with that," Susan said inside the kitchen. "Surely HomeFromHome can't let their guests behave like that."

"That fat bloke was this close to getting a slap," Colin said.

"You should have heard him last night," Henry said. "Drunk as a skunk he was and impossible to argue with."

"Have you seen the cars parked outside?" Susan said. "They're obviously not short of a bob or too."

"That doesn't mean anything," Henry said. "Wealth doesn't always translate to a good upbringing."

Rebecca placed a pot of tea on the table. "Let's not let them ruin this weekend. How about a drive to the sea?"

"We can get some fish and chips while we're there," Henry suggested. "And the twins can have a swim if they like."

"There's a lovely beach not far from here," Susan said. "I had a look on the internet last night. Katie and Paul have brought their swimming costumes."

Half an hour later they'd forgotten all about the obnoxious guests next door. They were heading west along the coast road in the direction of Highcliffe.

"Look at that," Colin nodded to the stretch of sand ahead of them.

Avon beach ran all the way from Mudeford in the east to where it joined up with Southbourne and ended up in Bournemouth.

"There's the beach, kids," Susan said.

For once the twins weren't glued to their phones. Katie and Paul gazed out of the window at the yellow sand up ahead.

"Can we get an ice cream?" Katie asked.

"It's expected of us," Rebecca replied. "You can't go to the beach without eating ice cream."

"And fish and chips," Henry reminded them.

"And fish and chips," Rebecca agreed.

Colin parked the Renault in the car park looking out to Southbourne Beach and everyone piled out. They walked past the row of colourful beach houses at the top and down the path through the overgrown vegetation towards the sand. It was a glorious early-May morning and the beach was already very busy. Umbrellas of all colours were dotted all around. The sea was calm and the surf was low.

"This is sublime," Henry commented. "Look at the colour of that water." The late-morning sun was not yet directly overhead, and the only clouds were innocuous white, fluffy ones that promised no harm. The beach was protected by natural breakwaters that ran the whole length of the sand. Every fifty metres or so these rocky jetties jutted out and created shallow pools that were safe to swim in. Children of all ages were scouring the pools for treasure. Shells and crabs and starfish were hauled up with fishing nets and placed in buckets of seawater. It truly was a tranquil scene.

Katie and Paul took off their T-Shirts and shorts and made their way towards the shore. Susan had suggested they put their swimming costumes on before they set off and now the twins were splashing around in the gentle waves. Alfred followed after them and soon the Jack Russell had joined them in the water.

They chose a spot not far from the shore on an even stretch of beach. Susan jammed a huge umbrella into the sand and opened it up. Henry spread his towel out, sat down and took out his book. After the disappointment of *Around the World in 80 Plays* he'd decided to play it safe today and he'd brought along one of his favourites. He'd read it many times before, but he always found something different in *Love in the time of Cholera*. He'd also discovered the effect it had on people around him when they read the cover and realised what he was reading. No, Gabriel Garcia

Marquez's masterpiece always seemed to ensure people gave Henry a wide berth while he was reading it. Alfred had decided he'd done enough exercise for the day – he flopped down by Henry's feet and was asleep in seconds.

Colin came and sat down next to him. "The twins are having a great time. It's nice to see them doing something outside for a change."

Henry looked up from his book. "You're welcome anytime. You know that."

"I keep thinking about the HomeFromHome rentals," Colin's tone turned serious. "There has to be something you can do about the nuisance they're causing."

"We've asked them to keep it down," Henry said. "What else can we do?"

"There must be something. They've been obnoxious and that fat bloke was downright abusive. You should report them to HomeFromHome."

"There's an email address where you can voice neighbourhood concerns," Susan said. "Loud music and abusive guests shouldn't be allowed."

"Not to mention the half-naked man and woman," Rebecca reminded them. "That's public indecency."

"Let's put it out of our minds for a bit," Henry suggested. "It's a lovely day and we can't let a bunch of rich hooligans ruin that for us."

The morning turned into afternoon. Henry put down his book and looked out to sea. The Isle of Wight stood proud in the distance. Katie and Paul had lost track of time and were now exploring the rock pools the tide had left behind. Colin and Susan had gone for a stroll along the beach and Rebecca had nodded off. Henry smiled as he listened to her heavy breathing.

"There's a lovely restaurant further up the beach," Colin said when he and Susan had returned from their walk. "It looks right out to sea."

"Do they serve fish and chips?" That was all Henry was concerned about.

"Of course," Susan said. "I'm getting a bit peckish, and I bet the twins are hungry too."

"Sounds good," Henry said. "You round up the kids and I'll see if I can wake up my wife."

They'd only walked a few hundred metres down the beach when Rebecca's phoned beeped to tell her she'd received a message. She took out her phone and saw she'd missed five calls from Phoebe.

"That's odd," she said. "I didn't hear it ring."

"There was no signal back there," Colin said.

"I'll see what she wants."

It turned out that Phoebe was in Frisk. She was parked outside Sea View Cottage, and she was wondering where everybody was.

"She's coming to join us," Rebecca said when she'd ended the call. "She was tearing her hair out at home and she decided to drive down to the cottage. It seems her and Len have broken up."

Henry shook his head. "I give up with that girl."

They found a table outside facing the beach. They ordered a round of drinks and decided to wait for Phoebe to get there before ordering the food. She walked in twenty minutes later and sat down next to Rebecca.

"You should have told us you were coming," Rebecca said.

"I tried to phone," Phoebe said.

"Signal was bad further down the beach," Colin said.

"Sorry about you and Len," Susan offered.

"I'm not," Phoebe said. "Turns out he was just like the rest of them, but I don't feel like going into it. Did you know the road outside the cottage looks like a car park?"

"There's some kind of reunion going on next door," Henry told her. "In the HomeFromHome place."

"I nearly had a fight with one of them," Colin said. "Fat little bastard who couldn't keep his mouth shut."

"They made a terrible din last night," Rebecca added. "That's one of the reasons we came down here."

"You can't let them chase you out of your own house," Phoebe said. "You should have phoned the police."

"Your mother did," Henry said. "But it seems times have changed. The police don't care about noisy neighbours anymore. It's now the responsibility of the council."

They all ordered fish and chips and it didn't take long for it to arrive. Henry held his beer in the air. "Cheers. Here's to many more days like these. This is the life."

"I'll drink to that," Rebecca agreed. "Life doesn't get much better than this."

## CHAPTER TWENTY THREE

Everyone was in high spirits as they set off back to Frisk. It had been a truly glorious day. It was now late afternoon and Rebecca was looking forward to a cup of tea and a few hours of relaxation in the garden. Katie and Paul were fast asleep on the back seat – the sun and sea air had clearly taken its toll on the twins. Phoebe had decided to stay the night. She didn't feel like driving back to London and Rebecca had suggested she sleep on the new sofa. Everybody was in a really good mood.

It didn't last long. Colin turned into Brightwater Lane, and everybody heard it. Even though the windows in the car were closed the drone of the bass speaker crept inside. As they got closer to Sea View Cottage the noise got louder and now the thud, thud of the music was accompanied by loud voices. Men and women were screaming and shouting, and it was clear that the reunion party was already in full swing.

Someone had parked in front of the gate to the cottage. A huge silver 4x4 was blocking the entrance.

"This has to stop," Rebecca said.

There were now at least fifteen cars parked along the road. Colin was forced to park twenty metres away from the cottage.

"I'll go and have a word," he said. "Tell them to move the car. They can't park in front of your property."

"I'll go," Phoebe offered. "I know you – you'll probably end up in a fight."

"I'll come with you," Susan said. "We can ask them to keep the noise down a bit too."

Henry woke the twins and they all walked up the road towards Sea View Cottage. The volume of the music was unbearable and Henry estimated there to be at least thirty people next door. Men and women were bellowing at each other. One woman was singing along to the music. She was clearly tone deaf.

"I'll put the kettle on," Henry said inside the cottage. "I hope the ladies can talk some sense into those hoodlums next door."

"This is unacceptable, dad," Colin said. "They're not allowed to make a din like that, no matter what time of day it is."

Susan and Phoebe came in. The music was still blaring from the speakers next door.

"The owner of the 4x4 is going to move it," Susan said. "But we didn't have any joy with the music. They've promised to turn it off at midnight."

"Midnight?" Henry said. "So, we've got to put up with this racket until midnight?"

"What else can we do?" Susan said. "You should see the speakers they've got next door. They're as big as a car."

"There's a couple of pretty nice-looking blokes there," Phoebe said. "One of them invited me to join them."

"You'll do no such thing," Henry said. "I will not have you fraternising with the enemy."

"Relax, Dad. Nobody is doing any fraternising here. You should see the huge bowl of punch they've made. I reckon there's going to be some thick heads in the morning."

"I've never seen such big speakers," Susan said.

"They're Bluetooth," Phoebe elaborated. "They must have cost a fortune."

"Bluetooth?" Rebecca repeated. "Of course. Why didn't I think of that before?"

"Think of what?" Henry asked.

"Don't you worry about it," Rebecca said with a grin on her face. "You just leave it up to me."

Henry was still none the wiser as he made the tea. He knew Rebecca was up to something – he'd seen that look on her face many times before, but he had no idea *what* she was up to. He put the pot of tea on a tray with some cups and brought it through to the living room. Rebecca was sitting at the table looking at something on her laptop.

"What are you doing?" Henry asked her.

"I need to download the latest Linux," Rebecca told him. "It's almost finished. We've got very strong Wi-fi here. OK, it's done. Let's see what they think about being knobbed by an old lady."

"Mum!" Colin exclaimed.

"Wash your mouth out with soap and water, mother" Phoebe added.

"It's an IT term," Rebecca explained. "A KNOB is the key negotiation of Bluetooth. Once I'm in I can force the Bluetooth speaker to use a weak encryption. If I'm right I can lower the entropy of the link to as little as one byte."

Henry frowned. "Does anyone have any idea what my wife just said?"

"She's going to hack the music, dad," Colin put it into layman's terms.

Rebecca carried on working. "Easy as pie. And the beauty of Linux is I don't have to pair with the other device and the owner of the device has no idea what I'm doing."

"You can take control of the speakers without them realising?" Colin said.

Rebecca grinned from ear to ear. "What shall we listen to?"

"Are you in?" Phoebe said. "Are you in control of the speakers next door?"

"I most certainly am."

"What about Postman Pat?" Phoebe suggested. "They'll love that."

Rebecca found a link, downloaded it and moments later the opening bars of the theme song to the popular children's series could be heard from next door. This was accompanied by a collective groan.

"That's brilliant, mum," Colin said.

"All those years at Higgins IT weren't wasted," Rebecca said. "And the beauty of hacking via Linux is they're not in control anymore. Even if they try and reboot the speakers – I hold the key, so they won't be able to get back in."

The music was turned off ten minutes later. The guests at the reunion had clearly had enough after having to endure Thomas the Tank Engine and Pingu.

Henry looked at his wife. "I thought you were in control of the speakers."

"I am," Rebecca said. "But only when they're turned on."

"They've switched them off," Phoebe said. "But if they put them on again mum will be able to choose what music plays out of them."

"I wonder if they've figured out what's going on," Colin said.

"I doubt it," Rebecca said. "Unless there's an IT expert among them. Let's go outside to the garden while we've got some peace and quiet."

Even though the music had stopped the noise from next door was still very loud. A few people had decided to make their own music and now the vulgar words of some kind of rugby song could be heard.

"We can't win," Henry said.

They sat around the table on the patio. Katie and Paul were playing games on the PC in the spare room. Alfred was snoring loudly on the sofa in the living room. Mrs Major was outside in her garden next door. The colonel's wife seemed oblivious to the raucous singing. She carried on pruning her roses, regardless.

A woman appeared at the fence and whistled to get their attention. Henry looked over at her, but he didn't get up. The woman whistled again.

"Can we help you?" Colin shouted to her.

"Have you lost your dog?" Henry asked.

"What?" the woman said.

"The way you whistled," Henry said. "I just assumed you were trying to get the attention of a dog."
"Have you got Wi-fi?"
"It comes and goes," Phoebe replied.
"Our Bluetooth isn't working. I was wondering if you had the same problem."
"Bluetooth?" Rebecca said.
"You use it to connect wirelessly. The speakers are playing up."
"I'm afraid that kind of thing is beyond me, love" Rebecca told her. "All this new technology gives me a headache."
"Sometimes we get kids messing around with the signal," Colin said with a face as deadpan as he could muster. "Especially on weekends."
"Bloody kids," Henry joined in.

A man appeared behind the woman.
"Philip has found a memory stick in his car," he told her. "His taste in music is crap but at least we'll have something to listen to."
With this, they both went to join the rest of the re-union guests. Soon afterwards the boom-boom of monotonous music could be heard.

"Well, that didn't last long," Rebecca said and sighed.
"I thought you could control it," Henry said.
"The USB sticks don't work wirelessly. There's nothing I can do about those."
"I hope it's not going to be like this every weekend," Henry said. "I'm starting to see what the angry man from across the road meant. This is enough to send anyone over the edge."
"I'm going to complain," Colin said.
"Leave it, Col," Rebecca told him. "You know what happened last time. You'll only end up causing more trouble."
"I'm going to complain to HomeFromHome."
"Get something on camera," Phoebe suggested. "They won't do anything without some kind of evidence to back it up."

After a few tries Colin admitted defeat. Each time he watched the playback on his phone he realised it didn't portray the true nature of the party next door.

"It doesn't look too bad on here," he said. "I doubt they'll take it seriously. It's a shame we didn't get footage of that fat bloke swearing at us."

"We should still complain, though," Susan said. "Just so they're aware of what goes on in these HomeFromHome rentals. You need to get all the neighbours to do the same. They can't ignore a whole bunch of complaints."

"It's worth a try," Colin said and brought up the HomeFromHome website on his phone.

"I'm going to do the same," Phoebe said.

"Me too," Susan joined in.

## CHAPTER TWENTY FOUR

It was starting to get dark and there was now a slight chill in the air. The change in the weather had made the guests next door move inside and the music wasn't so loud now.

"Thank God for that," Henry said. "Let's hope it rains for the rest of the weekend."

"Don't say that, dad," Phoebe said.

"If it means the animals next door calm down a bit, it can chuck it down as much as it likes as far as I'm concerned."

"I've had a reply from HomeFromHome," Colin said.

"That was quick," Susan said.

"They're just informing me they take neighbourhood concerns very seriously and they're looking into it."

"Good," Rebecca said. "Perhaps they'll tell the owner of number 12 to keep their guests under control."

An hour later something had changed next door. The volume was turned up and it was clear the party had moved back outside again. The same music as before was blasting out of the speaker. It was so loud the Green family were finding it hard to talk over the din.

"This is giving me a headache," Henry said.

Rebecca looked at the clock. It was two minutes past nine.

"If this is what it's going to be like every weekend, I don't think I'll be able to take it. We've still got three more hours of this racket."

Phoebe put on her coat and smiled. "You know what I've always said? If you can't beat 'em join 'em."

"You will do no such thing, Phoebe Green," Henry told her.

"Don't worry, dad," she said. "I've got a cunning plan."

"What are you going to do?" Colin asked.

"It's probably best you don't know. I shouldn't be long."

"What is that girl up to?" Henry asked when Phoebe had gone next door.

"I just hope she isn't falling back into her old habits," Rebecca said.

"She isn't," Colin said. "I've been keeping an eye on her and I would have noticed if she was on the drugs again. I know the signs."

"She seems to have got back on track," Susan agreed.

"What is she up to, then?" Henry said.

"I suppose we'll have to wait and see," Rebecca said.

The party was still in full swing next door. The noise from the reunion had got even louder. Phoebe's voice could be heard every now and then. The music blaring out of the speakers was so familiar now – everybody knew what song was coming next. It was as if the record was stuck and the music was on a continuous time loop.

"I'm going to see what's going on," Colin announced half an hour later. "Phoebe should have been back by now."

"What did that bloke say to her when you went there to ask them to move the car?" Rebecca asked Susan.

"He asked us to join them, but Phoebe gave him the brush-off. He wasn't even that good-looking."

"I just hope she knows what she's doing," Henry said. "It only takes a split second to lapse. I don't think I can go through that nonsense again."

"I'll go and take a look," Colin said and went outside to the back garden.

The scene playing out next door wasn't what Colin had expected. The music from the USB had finished and nobody had bothered to start it again. Colin had to look twice to make sure he was seeing what he thought he was seeing. There were bodies everywhere. On the lawn and outside on the patio bodies were strewn all over the place. Some of them were moving – others were groaning and some were clearly passed out. A man was helping a woman to her feet but he wasn't doing a very good job of it. They'd only made it a few feet when both of them collapsed in a heap next to another unconscious couple. Phoebe was nowhere to be seen. The unmistakable sound of someone vomiting could be heard nearby. All in all, it truly was a sight to behold.

Phoebe appeared behind Colin without him even realising she was there. He jumped when he felt her hand on his shoulder.

"Damn," he said. "You scared the daylights out of me. What have you done?"

Phoebe's eyes were sparkling. "Do you really want to know?"

"Probably not. What's wrong with all those people?"

"It's quiet, isn't it?"

"What did you do, Phoebe?"

"You can't tell mum and dad," Phoebe said. "Or Susan."

"What have you done, Phoebe?"

Phoebe put her hand in her pocket and took out a plastic bag. Inside were four or five green capsules.

"What the hell are those?" Colin asked.

"I came prepared," Phoebe told him. "I still know a few people and I brought something with me in case of emergencies."

"You're not using again, are you?"

"I'm insulted you even have to ask me that. No, but I thought the roofies might come in handy in situations like these."

"You drugged the guests with Rohypnol? For God's sake, Phoebe – you know that stuff is illegal. You've got a record – you could get into serious trouble for this."

"Relax, Col," Phoebe said. "Nobody knows it was me. There are thirty-odd yuppie types next door. Any one of them could have spiked that punch."

"Thirty-odd unconscious yuppie types," Colin reminded her. "I can't believe you did that. I thought they'd changed Rohypnol to make it impossible to spike drinks."

"It's got a blue dye added to it now, but in a bowl of luminous punch you can't even see it. I'd say that lot will be out of action for a good twelve hours, and when they do finally wake up they'll feel sick as dogs and won't even remember what happened to them."

Neither of them spoke for a while. Colin looked into the garden next door. Most of the guests were out cold now. Two women were staggering towards the house with their arms around each other. They'd barely made it inside when there was a loud crash and then silence.

Colin started to laugh. Phoebe looked at him and smiled, then she too started laughing.

"We can't mention this to anyone," Colin said.

"My lips are sealed," Phoebe agreed.

"I still can't believe you did that. How much did you put in that punch?"

"Enough. And I can promise you, these hooligans will not feel like a party tomorrow. I wouldn't be surprised if most of them went home early."

"You really are a piece of work, Phoebe Green."

"You know me," Phoebe said. "I'm just looking out for mum and dad. We won't mention a word of this ever again."

"Not a word."

"There's no harm done. Mum and dad get peace and quiet and nobody gets hurt in the process. Besides a headache to rival all headaches those guests will have no lasting side-effects."

## CHAPTER TWENTY FIVE

Rebecca woke to the sound of car doors slamming. She rubbed her eyes and realised it was still dark outside. Henry was snoring loudly next to her. The clock on the bedside table told her it was just before five in the morning. Another car door slammed, and the sound of voices could also now be heard. Rebecca sighed – the reunion next door had come to an abrupt halt at around ten the night before and she wondered if the guests had started again and were now calling it a night.

She got out of bed, making sure not to wake Henry and made her way down the corridor to the living room. It was in there where she realised something was wrong. The flashing lights and the occasional bleep of some kind of radio told her something had happened. She pushed the curtain to the side and saw two police cars and an ambulance parked outside in the road.

Susan came inside the room. She yawned and rubbed her eyes.
"What's going on?" she asked. "I woke up when I heard the car doors slamming."
"There's police cars and an ambulance outside," Rebecca told her. "Something must have happened next door."
"They finished the party early last night," Susan remembered. "I wonder what's happened?"
"I'm sure we'll soon find out. Cup of tea?"
"Thanks. I doubt I'll be able to get back to sleep now anyway."

Henry and Colin came into the living room an hour later. Both of them were deep sleepers and the commotion outside in the road hadn't disturbed them. Phoebe still hadn't stirred on the sofa.
"What's going on outside?" Henry asked.

"The police and an ambulance got here over an hour ago," Rebecca told him. "I think it's got something to do with the guests next door."

Colin walked over to the window and looked outside. Two paramedics were carrying something out of number 12. Colin froze when he realised what it was. It was a stretcher but from the way the body had been wrapped in a blue sheet from head to toe it was clear the only role the ambulance was going to play was in transporting the body to the morgue. One of the policemen in uniform spotted him and Colin instinctively stepped away from the window. He regretted it immediately.

Phoebe opened her eyes and stretched her arms wide. "What's going on?"

"We don't know," Henry told her. "Looks like something happened next door – the police and an ambulance are here."

"Is there any tea on the go?"

"I'll make you a cup," Susan offered.

"I'm going out to the back garden to get some fresh air," Colin said.

He caught Phoebe's eye and gave her a slight, sidewards nod of his head to indicate he wanted her to join him.

"This is bad, Phoebe," Colin said outside.

"We don't know what happened yet," she said.

"Someone died. I saw them bringing out the body. How much of that drug did you actually put in the punch?"

"Whoa," Phoebe said. "Hold your horses, Col. We don't know if this is anything to do with that. I only emptied a dozen or so capsules into it. Just enough to knock them out for a bit. Roofies aren't dangerous."

"All I know is someone was just brought out in a body bag. And the police are going to be asking questions."

Phoebe shrugged. "Let them. They can't prove I had anything to do with it. It could have been any one of them that spiked that punch."

"You were there last night, Phoebe," Colin reminded her. "Someone might tell the police that."
"I doubt it. One of the things about Rohypnol is the memory loss it causes. I should know. Most of those people won't even remember anything about what happened last night. We've got nothing to worry about."
"Someone died. Doesn't that bother you?"
"People die all the time. There's probably a perfectly good explanation for it, and I doubt the police will even bother coming here."

* * *

They'd just finished clearing away the dishes later that afternoon when the doorbell rang. Colin, Phoebe and Susan were sitting outside in the back garden. Rebecca opened the door to a man and a woman. The man looked to be in his mid-forties - he was short and stocky and the woman was much younger. She was slim and tall and her green eyes were full of suspicion. She looked Rebecca up and down then her eyes came to rest on Rebecca's face.
"Can I help you?" Rebecca asked her.
"DI Reece," she said. "And this is DS Bright. We're from Bournemouth CID. Can we have a word? Mrs?"
"Green. Rebecca Green."
"Mrs Green," DS Bright said. "This shouldn't take long."
"CID?" Rebecca repeated. "Sounds serious. I suppose you'd better come in."

She led them into the living room. "Would you like something to drink? Tea or coffee?"
"No, thank you," DI Reece replied.
"Take a seat," Rebecca said. "This is my husband, Henry. I assume this about what happened next door."
Henry shifted Alfred from the three-seater sofa. "What exactly did happen next door?"

The Jack Russell didn't look impressed. He stretched his legs and padded off to the kitchen.

"We're not sure yet," DI Reece said and sat down.

Her colleague sat in the spot on the sofa recently vacated by Alfred.

"How long have you lived here in Frisk?" DS Bright asked.

"Almost a week," Henry replied.

DI Reece raised an eyebrow. "A week?"

"We've recently moved from London," Rebecca said. "It all happened so quickly. We sold our house in Wimbledon and moved here."

"Why are you asking how long we've lived here?" Henry said.

"I'm just curious," DI Reece said. "The cottage next door is a HomeFromHome rental, is that right?"

"Half of the places in the street are," Rebecca said.

"And you have no problem with that?"

"Why should we? People are allowed to go on holiday, aren't they?"

"Yes, they are. Is it just the two of you living here?"

"That's right," Rebecca said.

"I see. So, there's nobody else here?"

"We've got our daughter, and our son and his family here for the bank holiday weekend."

"You said there was just the two of you," DS Bright said.

"No," Henry said. "What my wife said was there were two of us living here. It was in direct response to DI Reece's question. You need to be more specific in your questions. My wife and I live here, and our family are visiting for the long weekend. Does that clarify things?"

A brief smile appeared on DI Reece's face. "I apologise, Mr Green. I'll try to be more unequivocal in the future."

"I'd appreciate that," Henry said.

"We believe there was some kind of school reunion happening next door," DI Reece said.

"Apparently," Rebecca said. "We asked them to keep the noise down but they didn't listen."

"We did call the police," Henry added. "But it appears the police have better things to do than listen to the woes of homeowners whose lives are being made unbearable by HomeFromHome guests. One of them swore at me."

"And another threatened our Col," Rebecca added.

"And the police couldn't give a hoot," Henry said.

"I'm very sorry about that, Mr Green," DI Reece said. "Unfortunately, resources are tight within the police as a whole. We cannot spare the resources to respond to every call about noisy neighbours."

"And yet these sparse resources seem to stretch to sending a couple of detectives out to talk to two pensioners in riddles. What exactly is going on here?"

"OK, Mr Green," DI Reece said. "I'll tell you what is going on here. No doubt news will get out soon enough anyway. Something happened next door during that reunion party. Something that resulted in nine people being rushed to hospital."

"Three of them didn't make it, Mr Green," DS Bright added. "One was dead before the ambulance even got here, and two more died soon afterwards. Three of those guests are dead."

## CHAPTER TWENTY SIX

Henry and Rebecca sat in the back garden looking out at the Solent in the distance. Everything was quiet – the guests had gone, the police had gone, and the silence was somewhat unsettling after the chaos of the past few days. Colin, Phoebe and Susan had taken a walk down to the Frisk Arms for a few drinks and the twins were playing games on the computer.

The visit from the two Bournemouth detectives had unnerved Henry and Rebecca. Three of the guests from the reunion were dead and DI Reece and DS Bright had suggested their deaths were suspicious. Those three people hadn't died of natural causes.

Rebecca sipped her tea. "I didn't like what those detectives were implying back there. They think we had something to do with the deaths of those people."

"Don't be silly, love," Henry said. "How could we be involved in the deaths of three people we didn't even know?"

"It's like they knew things, but they weren't letting on about it."

"That's how detectives operate," Henry assured her. "Those two were straight out of a crime novel. The pair of them were nothing but stereotypes. I don't know why they don't just come straight out and ask the questions they want the answers to. Why do they always have to mask their true intentions with vague comments? They're hackneyed, predictable robots. And I can't see the point in this *we'll probably need to speak to you again*, twaddle. If they're so sure they'll want to speak to us again, why not do it now and save time? No, they moan about their precious resources – they wouldn't have that problem if they were taught how to formulate their questions properly. I wouldn't worry about it – they won't be back."

Alfred came outside, did what he needed to do and went back in. A sound to the side made Rebecca look around. Mary Major was standing by the fence with a pair of pruning shears in her hands.

"Hello there," Rebecca shouted to her even though she wasn't sure the colonel's wife could hear her.

"Hello," Mary shouted back.

She was obviously wearing her hearing aids.

"Would you like to join us for a cup of tea?" Henry asked. "Kettle's not long boiled."

"That would be lovely," Mary said. "I could do with a break. The roses have been quite a handful this year."

"The front door's open," Rebecca said. "Let yourself in."

Mary emerged from the back door and sat down next to Rebecca. Henry placed a fresh pot of tea on the table.

"Did you hear what happened next door?" He asked Mary

"I've only just put my aids back in," she said. "But I did see the police and the ambulance."

"Did they not speak to you?" Rebecca said.

"Why would they speak to me?"

"Three people died," Henry said. "We had two detectives from Bournemouth round earlier asking questions."

"Oh my. Do they know what happened?"

"They wouldn't tell us," Rebecca said. "And I don't know how they thought we could help them."

"The truth will come out in the end," Mary said. "It always does. I love those rhododendrons. Not many people know how to look after them properly."

"I always thought it was illegal to plant them," Henry said.

"You can plant them," Mary said. "But you have to make sure they don't spread to the wild. They're an invasive species."

"Much like the guests at the HomeFromHome rentals," Henry quipped.

Mary laughed. "I'm going to enjoy having you as neighbours."

"What were the previous owners of Sea View Cottage like?" Rebecca asked.

"Lily and Peter? We didn't speak much. They kept themselves to themselves and Lily spent most of the time confined to bed in the last few months."

"What happened to her?" Rebecca said. "I mean how did she die?"

"Nerves, according to Peter. And he went the same way soon afterwards."

"Mr King across the road reckons the guests sent them to an early grave," Henry said.

"Ah yes," Mary said. "Mr King. He's a strange one, that one. But he could be right about those guests. I'm lucky to be able to switch the world off – I imagine it must be unbearable to have to endure that every weekend."

Alfred came outside and flopped at Mary's feet.

"He likes you," Henry said. "Alfie is a good judge of character."

"The colonel loved dogs," Mary said. "We always had a dog, but when he passed I didn't think I'd have long left myself, so I never got another one. It's not fair, is it? To leave an animal behind, I mean? In hindsight, I could have had many years with a dog by my side, but I never thought I'd be here this long."

"Hindsight is a wonderful thing," Henry said. "It's just a shame it always occurs too late."

Rebecca looked over the fence into number 12. The evidence of the reunion was still very much apparent. Bottles and cans were littered all over the garden – two of the outside chairs were laid on their side in one of the flower beds and the rose bushes at the end had been flattened. Dawson's Cleaning was going to have their work cut out when they came to clean up.

"Do you know the owners of number 12?" Rebecca asked Mary.

"I've never met them," Mary replied. "But I believe the same person owns 12, 14 and 16."

"I wonder how we can find out about them," Henry said. "See if we can reason with them about the behaviour of their guests."

"I would think three dead bodies in one of their HomeFromHome rentals would be rather bad for business," Mary said.

"Hmm," Rebecca said. "I imagine it would be extremely bad for business."

## CHAPTER TWENTY SEVEN

Detective Inspector Catherine Reece was exhausted. She was also deeply concerned. Two men and a woman had died in a HomeFromHome rental in Frisk. There had been thirty-one people attending the reunion and most of them claimed to have no memory of what happened the previous night. Those who could tell DI Reece anything had been rather vague and their versions of events didn't quite tally. It was all very confusing.

"What exactly happened there last night?" DI Reece asked the screen of her laptop.

She'd been informed that cause of death was going to take time. There was no obvious sign of foul play, and the few people they'd spoken to couldn't remember anything that could possibly explain why three of the party guests were no longer alive.

DI Reece's initial suspicion was that the fatalities were caused by some kind of drug overdose but none of the people who'd been interviewed could confirm this. One of the dead men, Fredrick Fisher was known to the police – he had a record for dealing going back to the late-nineties, but according to everyone they'd spoken to that was ancient history. Fisher had kept his nose clean since that one arrest and DI Reece knew instinctively that particular lead was a dead end.

All three of the fatalities were at school together. That part was obvious - they were attending a school reunion, but until they'd dug a bit deeper there was no way of knowing if they were linked in any other way. DI Reece didn't believe this was important either. She didn't think the link between the dead people was relative to the investigation but she didn't know exactly what was relevant. It was all very baffling and in her six years in CID it was one of the strangest cases she had ever come across. They had three dead bodies – a long list of potential witnesses, but most of those witnesses had no recollection of what went on at the party. They had no evidence of foul play – no sign of forced entry or a struggle taking place and it occurred to DI Reece the only thing they were certain of was the hearts of three people had stopped beating at roughly the same time. They had so little to go on DI Reece wasn't even sure where the initial focus of the investigation should lie. She didn't know where to look first.

Then she'd thought about something two of the people they'd interviewed *had* remembered. There had been a guest at the party who wasn't part of the reunion. Someone who hadn't been in the class of '89 was also there and when DI Reece dug further a spark of hope was ignited.

Phoebe Green had been arrested ten years ago for possession and intent to supply. She'd been caught when the police in Wimbledon raided a nightclub. Phoebe received a suspended sentence with terms and conditions attached and she'd spent time in a rehabilitation centre. It wasn't much to go on – Phoebe wasn't a big player in the greater scheme of things, but it was a lead, nevertheless. And among the drugs Phoebe was caught with that night was a benzodiazepine called Flunitrazepam. The police had seized more than a hundred capsules of the drug. The sedative went under various names – roofies, roopies, forget-me-pill, mind-eraser to name a few but DI Reece was well aware of some of the side-effects of Rohypnol. Memory loss was one of those.

And now DI Catherine Reece had made up her mind where her focus in the investigation was going to lie. She realised they needed to look more closely at Phoebe Green.

* * *

Phoebe finished the wine in her glass and stood up. "One more round?" Colin drained his beer glass and handed it to her. "Might as well. I'm not looking forward to going back to the cottage after the visit from the police."

"They were just doing a routine door-to-door," Susan insisted. "They do that in all suspicious deaths. They do in the crime thriller books, anyway. It doesn't mean they suspect you of anything. How could they?"

"I'll get the drinks in," Phoebe said.

"What's wrong with you?" Susan asked Colin. "You've been acting strange since the visit from the police."

"What do you expect?" Colin said. "Three people die next door to mum and dad and then the police come round asking questions."

"I wonder how they died," Susan said. "One death can be explained – especially where excess alcohol is involved, but for three people to die at the same time is really odd."

"I suppose we'll find out sooner or later."

Phoebe returned with the drinks. She placed them on the table and looked at Colin and Susan.

"What's with the long faces? We're supposed to be enjoying the long weekend."

"It's those three dead guests," Susan said. "It's just quite a shock, that's all."

"At least mum and dad won't have to put up with the noise tonight."

"What's wrong with you?" Colin asked. "Don't you care that three people are dead?"

"People die all the time. Why should I lose sleep over three dead strangers?"

Colin glared at her. "Maybe you should."

"Come on," Susan said. "Fighting about it isn't going to help. Let's try and forget about it – it's not like it was our fault they died."

"Do you think the HomeFromHome will be closed down?" Phoebe asked.

"I doubt it," Susan replied. "Just because there was a tragedy there doesn't mean people will stop coming."

"Some people actually get a kick out of it," Phoebe said. "There are weirdoes out there who get off on visiting places where people have died."

Colin was about to comment on this when his mobile phone started to ring. He looked at the screen.

"It's mum."

He answered the phone and after a few seconds he handed it to Phoebe.

"She wants to talk to you."

Phoebe took the phone. "Hi, mum. Is everything alright?"

"Are you still at the pub?" Rebecca asked.

"That's right."

"The police were here again. That woman DI wants to speak to you."

Phoebe frowned. "What for?"

"Someone told her you were at the party last night."

"I was there for half an hour," Phoebe said.

"The detective was rather vague, but she's on her way to the Frisk Arms now. I just wanted to warn you."

"It's probably just routine," Phoebe said. "She probably just wants to ask me some questions about what went on. Thanks for the warning."

"Is everything alright?" Colin asked when Phoebe had ended the call.

"The police want to speak to me," Phoebe said. "About the party last night. Someone told them I was there for a bit."

"Shit." The word came out before Colin could stop himself.

Susan turned to look at him. "Is there something you're not telling me?"

Colin didn't get the chance to reply. The door to the pub opened and DI Reece and DS Bright came in. They spotted Phoebe and walked over to the table.

"I don't know what you think I can tell you," Phoebe got in first. "I was at the party for just over half an hour. And I promise you, everyone was fine when I left."

DI Reece nodded. "Could you come with us, please?"

"What's going on?" Susan asked.

"Could you come with us, please?" DS Bright said.

"Are you arresting her?" Colin said.

"We'd just like to ask Miss Green some questions," DI Reece said.

"Do I need to phone a lawyer?" Colin said.

"That's entirely up to you, Mr Green."

"Don't bother," Phoebe said and stood up. "This won't take long." She looked at DI Reece. "Shall we go?"

## CHAPTER TWENTY EIGHT

"Interview with Phoebe Rebecca Green commenced 20:15," DI Reece began. "Sunday, May 5th 2019. Present, Miss Green, DI Reece and DS Bright. For the record Miss Green has waived her right to legal representation. Miss Green..."

"Would you mind calling me Phoebe?" Phoebe interrupted. "I'm almost forty and Miss Green makes me sound like a real loser."

"Phoebe," DI Reece said. "As you wish. Do you understand why you're here?"

"I assume it's because I spent a bit of time at the party last night."

"The school reunion," DS Bright elaborated. "It was the Grey Comprehensive class of '89 reunion."

"You didn't attend Grey Comp, did you?" It was DI Reece.

"I was ten-years-old in 1989," Phoebe said.

"That's a no then. What were you doing at the party if you weren't part of the reunion?"

"Someone had parked in front of my mum and dad's cottage," Phoebe explained. "My sister-in-law and I went to ask them to move the car and while we were there this bloke asked me to join the party."

"I see. Your parents live next door, is that correct?"

"They've just moved into Sea View Cottage."

"We have witnesses who've testified that some kind of altercation took place between some of your family and a few of the guests," DI Reece continued. "Is that correct?"

"They were making quite a din next door," Phoebe said. "And we asked them to turn it down a bit. One of the reunion party got very abusive. He swore at us."

"And yet you still took this man up on his offer of joining them?" DS Bright said. "That's a bit odd, don't you think?"

"I like a good knees-up as much as the next person," Phoebe said. "And I don't mind a bit of loud music, so I popped in for a bit."

"Even though your parents weren't happy about the noise? I understand they actually called the police to report the disturbance."

"They're pensioners. They came here for some peace and quiet. And they weren't being unreasonable when they asked the guests to keep it down a bit. Why exactly am I here? I told you, I went next door for thirty-odd minutes and that was it. I don't know what else I can tell you."

"You've been in trouble with the police before, haven't you?" DI Reece said.

"Is that what this is all about?" Phoebe said. "I'm a suspect because of one stupid mistake a long time ago? There were thirty-odd people there last night, and I bet I'm not the only one who has made a mistake."

"No," DI Reece said. "You're not. Can you tell us why you were arrested?"

"It was ten years ago," Phoebe said. "A stupid mistake, that's all."

"You were arrested for possession and intent to supply," DS Bright said. "Is that right?"

"You've clearly seen my record. I went to rehab and I haven't been anywhere near drugs since. Ten years is a long time."

"You were caught with over a hundred tabs of Rohypnol, isn't that right?" DI Reece said. "Are you familiar with the drug?"

"Of course, I am."

"So, you know all about the side-effects. More than half of the guests we spoke to have no recollection of what happened last night."

"They were all very drunk," Phoebe said.

"Memory loss is one of the common side-effects of Rohypnol," DS Bright said.

"Do you want to know what I think happened last night?" DI Reece said.
"I suppose you're going to tell me anyway."
"I think the reason for those people being unable to recall the events of last night is this: Somehow, they ingested a drug similar to Rohypnol. The few witness statements we did get suggest this. One minute the reunion guests were up and about and the next they were dropping like flies. And the next day hardly any of them could remember what happened. Those that did not ingest the drug were able to confirm the condition of those who we suspect did."
"And you think I had something to do with it?" Phoebe asked.
"We're just crossing things off the list at this stage," DI Reece said. "We'll know soon enough how those three people died."

"Is this going to take much longer?" Phoebe asked. "I do actually have better things to do."
"I imagine you do," DI Reece said.
"Look," Phoebe said. "I don't know what else I can tell you. Why would I want to kill three people? I have absolutely no reason to kill anybody."
"I don't doubt that."
"Then what am I doing here?"
"Three people are dead," DS Bright said. "Six more are still in hospital and that tends to make us suspicious. When that happens, we like to do things thoroughly. We leave no stone unturned."
"Well, you're not going to find anything under this particular stone. I have no idea how those people died and that's all I can tell you."

"Interview with Phoebe Rebecca Green ended, 20:34," DI Reece said.
"Thank you for your time, Miss Green and I apologise for any inconvenience it may have caused. Will you be staying in the area long?"
"I'm heading back to London tomorrow," Phoebe told her. "I have to be back at work on Tuesday."

"We'll need your contact details in London," DS Bright said.

"Just in case we need to talk to you again," DI Reece added.

"Of course," Phoebe said. "I've got nothing to hide."

"DS Bright will give you a lift back to Frisk," DI Reece said. "Sorry again for any inconvenience."

## CHAPTER TWENTY NINE

"What did they say?" Colin asked Phoebe.

DS Bright had dropped her off a few minutes earlier and she and Colin were sitting outside in the back garden.

"They found out about my past," she told him. "They always jump on the ones with form first – it's just how they operate."

"Did you get the impression they know what happened?"

"The woman DI is a sharp cookie," Phoebe said. "She figured out some kind of benzo was involved from what the witnesses told her. That's why I was hauled in. The first thing they do is check to see if anyone has a record."

"This is serious shit, Phoebe."

"They can't prove anything. Unless somebody saw me spike that punch, they've got nothing."

"What did you do with the rest of the Rohypnol?"

"What do you think?" Phoebe said. "I got rid of it as soon as the police came calling. Flushed the whole lot down the toilet."

"Good."

"They won't find anything that links me to those deaths," Phoebe assured him.

"Let's hope they don't," Colin said. "Let's hope for your sake someone doesn't suddenly remember something."

"Come on, Col," Phoebe put her hand on his shoulder. "Any testimony given later will be thrown straight out. The roofies will make the statements unreliable – I know from experience how Rohypnol works. I don't think we've got anything to worry about."

Rebecca appeared in the kitchen doorway. Phoebe wasn't sure how long she'd been standing there.

"What are you two talking about?" she asked and sat down at the table with them.
"Phoebe's interrogation," Colin said.
"About that," Rebecca looked at her daughter. "Why were they so keen to interview you?"
"Because of what happened ten years ago," Phoebe told her. "They ran a check, found out about my record and hauled me in."
"They always do that," Colin assured his mother. "It's standard procedure."
"It'd done and dusted," Phoebe said. "I had nothing to tell them, and they soon realised that. Where's dad?"
"Supposedly reading. Although how anyone can read with their eyes closed is beyond me. He's snoring like a chainsaw on the sofa. What time do you have to be off tomorrow?"
"Not early," Phoebe said. "We can make the most of the long weekend."
"I thought we could take a drive to Bournemouth," Rebecca suggested. "Your dad's not too keen but the twins will love it."
"Sounds like a plan."

"What are you doing for your birthday?" Colin asked his mother.
"I hadn't really thought about it," Rebecca said. "It's not a big birthday anyway."
She was turning sixty-three the following week.
"It's your first birthday in the cottage," Phoebe said. "You have to do something special."
"When you get to my age a birthday isn't a thing to celebrate," Rebecca said. "Me and your father will probably just have a quiet meal at home."
"Nonsense," Colin said. "You'll do no such thing. We'll have to organise something nice."

He stood up. "Arsenal are playing in a minute so I'll leave you ladies to it."

"Who are they playing?" Phoebe asked.

"Brighton. Should be a walk in the park for the Gunners."

With that he went inside the kitchen.

"Right, Phoebe Green," Rebecca said. "Are you going to tell me what really happened last night?"

Her tone of voice and serious expression told Phoebe it would be pointless lying to her mother.

"How long were you standing in the doorway?" Phoebe asked. "How much did you hear?"

"Enough," Rebecca said. "Out with it."

"Are you sure dad's asleep"

"He's dead to the world. He can't hear us. I want to know everything."

Phoebe sighed a long sigh. "It wasn't supposed to turn out like it did. They were just supposed to pass out. I never meant anyone to die."

"What exactly did you do?"

"I just mixed some drugs in the punch they were all drinking. Just enough to knock them out for a bit."

"Oh, Phoebe," Rebecca said. "What have you done?"

"I didn't set out to kill anyone."

"I know you didn't. What do the police know?"

"I really don't know. The woman DI suspects some kind of benzo was used but unless someone saw me spike the punch, she can't link it to me."

"Did anyone see you?"

"I don't think so," Phoebe said. "The roofies have a habit of erasing the memory and making everything rather hazy so I don't think anyone will recall me putting the drugs in the punch."

"Good," Rebecca said. "That's good."

"And I got rid of the rest of the drugs."

"Where did you even get them?"

"I still know people," Phoebe said. "And before you ask, I'm not using again."

"I wasn't going to ask. This is what we're going to do. Should the police come back again, we're going to deny any knowledge of those drugs. Deny, deny, deny. Who else knows about this?"

"Just you and Colin," Phoebe said. "And Col won't say anything. I didn't mean any harm – I was just looking out for you and dad."

"I know you were. I think we should all try and put this behind us. Like you say, the police can't prove we had anything to do with it so we'll leave it at that."

"I'm sorry, mum," Phoebe said. "I'm sorry this had to happen in your first week at the cottage."

"It's alright, love," Rebecca put her hand on Phoebe's shoulder. "Your intentions were good and what's done is done. Let's put it all behind us."

Rebecca had no intention of putting it behind her. Phoebe's actions had stirred something up inside. A spark had been ignited and the kindling of a fire was now burning deep within.

# CHAPTER THIRTY

The following week was spent putting the finishing touches to the cottage. A leather sofa bed was delivered early in the week and was now inside the small study. Three book shelves had also been ordered and they arrived a day later. After much huffing and puffing Henry had managed to assemble them and fix them to the wall.

"Why is it you have to build everything yourself these days?" he'd complained.

"Most things come in a flat pack in this day and age," Rebecca had explained.

"It's ridiculous. In the old days you'd order a book shelf or a TV unit and that's what would be delivered – not a load of planks of wood and a bunch of random screws and bolts. Not to mention the badly-written instructions on how to assemble the bloody things. I reckon the day is not far off when you'll buy a car and have to build it yourself before you can drive it."

By the time he'd filled the shelves with his prized books he'd calmed down a bit. The study was taking shape and Henry was feeling rather pleased with himself. Here was a space he could come and read in peace. With his books arranged alphabetically he could imagine many pleasurable hours inside this room in the future.

It was Rebecca's birthday the next day and Colin, Susan and the twins were coming down for the weekend. Phoebe wasn't sure if she'd have to work but she promised to try and make it sometime over the weekend.

The detectives from Bournemouth hadn't put in another appearance and Rebecca was hoping that was the end of it. If they'd found something new they would have been in touch by now. Rebecca had thought long and hard about what Phoebe had done and some nights she'd been unable to sleep. Three of the guests at the HomeFromHome rental had lost their lives and

Rebecca couldn't stop wondering if this was all part of something much bigger. Surely the fact that the deaths of the guests coincided with Rebecca and Henry moving to Sea View Cottage should be seen as some kind of sign. Rebecca had always been an advocate of fate – there were some aspects of life that were mapped out well in advance and it was pointless trying to fight them. And the package she found on the mat next to the front door the next morning only served to confirm this.

It was the day of Rebecca's sixty-third birthday and she'd risen early. Henry and Alfred were engaged in a snoring competition in the bedroom and Rebecca had left them to it. She spotted the package out of the corner of her eye when she was on her way to the kitchen to make some tea. It was roughly seven inches by four inches and it had been wrapped in brown paper. When Rebecca picked it up she could tell straight away it was a book. There was no stamp or postmark on the package – it had been hand posted. On the front a simple message had been written in black, block capitals.

HAPPY BIRTHDAY, REBECCA. I SAW THIS AND THOUGHT OF YOU.

MARY.

Intrigued, Rebecca began to tear away at the brown paper. She opened it up and looked at the cover of the book. It was a photograph of a strange-looking frog. Its body was luminous orange, with bold black markings dotted here and there and its front and back legs were a mottled grey colour. Rebecca read the title and frowned.

*Poisons and Poisonings – Death by Stealth.*

She couldn't figure out why the colonel's wife had given her this book for her birthday. She didn't have time to dwell on the thought when the sound of the toilet flushing told her Henry was up and about. Without thinking she took the book to the living room, opened the sideboard and stuffed it behind a file used to keep a record of household expenses. Henry never looked at these files and Rebecca knew the book would remain hidden.

"What are you doing?" Henry asked as Rebecca closed the sideboard door.

"I couldn't sleep," Rebecca said. "So, I did a bit of household paperwork."

"You and your filing," Henry said.

"I like to keep on top of things. Cup of tea?"

"I'll make it," Henry offered. "You're not lifting a finger today. Hold on. Stay right where you are."

He left the room without further explanation.

He returned a short while later with a box wrapped in Christmas wrapping paper.

"It was the only wrapping paper I could find. Happy birthday, love."

He gave her a peck on the cheek. "Open it, then."

Rebecca undid the ribbon on the top and carefully tore off the wrapping paper. She opened the lid and saw that all the box contained was a small envelope.

"What's this?" Rebecca asked. "And why did you need such a big box?"

"It was our Phoebe's idea," Henry said. "She said it would confuse you. Open the envelope."

Rebecca opened it, read what was written on the sheet of paper inside and a smile appeared on her face.

"Oh, Henry. I love it. This is the best present I've ever been given."

"Our Col found the place on the net," Henry said. "It's a garden centre just outside Milford and it's got everything according to the website. Like it says on the note – the sky's the limit. I didn't have a clue what to get you after all these years and this way you can get exactly what you want for the garden."

"I love it," Rebecca said once more. "The sky's the limit, you say?"

"Within reason," Henry said. "Within reason, of course."

Henry made tea and a breakfast of bacon and scrambled eggs and they ate it outside on the patio. It was a glorious mid-May morning and it boded well for what Henry had in store. He planned to drag the barbecue out and treat Rebecca and the family to a barbecue like no other. He'd invited Mary from next door and Henry was determined to make Rebecca's first birthday in Sea View Cottage one she would remember for a very long time. Colin, Susan and the twins were due to arrive in an hour or so and Phoebe had called the night before to let them know she would be coming down later that afternoon.

Henry cleared the plates from the table on the patio and took them to the kitchen. Rebecca was already busy making plans for the garden. Her birthday present from Henry told her she could buy whatever she wanted from the garden centre and now Rebecca was mapping out where everything would go.

Henry was about to make a start on the dishes when he heard the sound of a car door being slammed outside in the road. He turned off the water and went to see if Colin and Susan had got there early.

It wasn't Colin's Renault parked outside, but the blue Mercedes Benz looked vaguely familiar. When Henry spotted the man standing outside the house belonging to Lionel King from number 11 he remembered where he'd seen the car before. The man was extremely tall and his giraffe-like neck seemed even longer today. Darren Needham was talking on his mobile phone outside Lionel King's cottage. Another man appeared, opened the boot of the car and took something out.

Henry watched with keen interest what he did next. He walked over to the gate that opened on to the path to the front door. Then he took out a handful of cable ties and attached the *For Sale* sign to the gate.

## CHAPTER THIRTY ONE

Henry lit the barbecue and coughed when a waft of smoke from the pungent firelighters hit him in the face. Colin, Susan and the twins had arrived an hour earlier, and they were all in the back garden. Rebecca was next door with Mary Major. Henry smiled – Rebecca and the colonel's wife had become good friends since they moved to Frisk.

Henry couldn't stop thinking about what he'd seen earlier. Why was Lionel King from number 11 putting his cottage on the market? And what was Darren Needham doing there? From the moment he laid eyes on the lanky estate agent Henry had been filled with a fierce sense of distrust. There was something very off about Darren Needham.

Henry had always had a curious nature and the *For Sale* sign outside number 11 was really bugging him.

"Could you watch the barbecue for me, son?" he said to Colin. "There's something I need to do."

"No problem," Colin said. "Where are you going?"

"I'm just popping across the road. It's time we got to know the neighbours."

"Where's Henry gone?" Susan asked Colin.

Colin added some more charcoal to the barbecue. "He was a bit vague. How many of us are there?"

"Seven," Susan said. "Including Phoebe. She should be here soon."

"I'd better stick some more charcoal on then."

That number increased to nine when Henry came back. He was with a short, stout man and a very thin woman. Henry had decided to invite Lionel King and his wife Diana to the barbecue. It had taken a bit of persuading but in the end Lionel had agreed to join them for an hour or so. Henry's intentions weren't exactly altruistic – he had no desire to spend much time with the angry old man from across the road, but he was curious about why

Lionel had put his house on the market and he was determined to get some answers.

Diana King was a frail woman with thinning grey hair. Lionel's hand was constantly attached to her shoulder and Henry wondered what would happen if he let go. Would she fall to the ground without her husband propping her up? The sallow skin on her face was stretched tightly over her cheekbones and this made her eye sockets appear unnaturally large. Her pale blue eyes were cloudy and lifeless and she sighed almost continuously. All in all, she was a rather wretched-looking woman. Lionel, on the other hand looked fit and well. His ruddy complexion suggested he spent a lot of time outdoors and, besides the permanent scowl on his face he appeared to be in good health.

"This is Lionel and Diana from across the road," Henry introduced them to Colin and Susan.

Lionel nodded to them and looked around the garden. "Still needs a bit of work, I see."

"Are you a gardener?" Susan asked him.

"I like to get my hands dirty."

"How long have you lived in Frisk?" Colin said.

Lionel ignored him and turned to Henry. "I think Diana needs to sit down."

Henry had brought some extra chairs outside and placed them around the table. They were impossible to miss.

"Do you have something more comfortable?" Lionel asked. "Those look rather hard."

"I'll fetch a cushion from the living room," Colin offered.

He went inside before Lionel could argue.

Phoebe came outside. The first thing she did was look over the fence into the garden of number 12. The cottage next door had been quiet since the incident with the reunion guests.

"Hello, love," Henry said. "How was the drive?"

"Uneventful," Phoebe replied. "Where's mum?"

"Next door with the colonel's wife. This is Lionel and his wife, Diana."

Phoebe looked Lionel King up and down then she looked at her father. The last time she'd seen Lionel was outside on the road and he hadn't exactly made a good impression on her.

"We've met," she said to Lionel. "Pleased to meet you, Diana."

Lionel's wife sighed deeply by way of a reply.

Colin came out with a couple of cushions. "These should make the chair more comfortable, Mrs King. Where shall I put them?"

Lionel yanked the bigger one from his hands. "I'll do it. I know what she likes."

Colin didn't object. Instead, he walked over to the fence. Phoebe followed him.

"Have you heard any more from the police?" Colin asked.

"Two local plods came to see me earlier in the week. They were asking questions about the reunion party again but it was obvious they were just trying to rattle me a bit. If they'd found something new they would have taken me in. I think I'm in the clear. The police will probably put it down to accidental death. There's no way they're going to link me to that punch bowl."

"And my lips are sealed," Colin said. "We're the only ones who know what really happened."

"Mum knows."

"What the hell?"

"She heard us talking, Col," Phoebe said. "I had to tell her."

"Shit. What did she say?"

"She told me to put it behind me. Forget all about it."

"Do you think she's told anybody else?"

"Of course not," Phoebe said. "Who would she tell?"

"I don't know. Mum's always been broad-minded, but this is a different kettle of fish altogether, Phoebe. You were responsible for the deaths of three people. I'm not sure mum will be able to put that kind of thing behind her just like that."

"Mum won't tell a soul," Phoebe insisted. "She promised me. Can we talk about something else?"

## CHAPTER THIRTY TWO

Phoebe wasn't aware there *was* someone else who knew about what happened to the reunion guests. Earlier that day Mary Major had caught Rebecca's attention in the garden and told her they needed to talk. Rebecca had told Henry Mary wanted to show her something in the garden and now the two ladies were sipping tea in the colonel's wife's kitchen.

"I know everything."

This took Rebecca by surprise. "How? How can that be possible?"

Mary tapped her ear. "Without my aids in I may as well have concrete in my ears, but when I turn them right up, I can hear better than anyone. I heard everything. I was out in the garden and I overheard your son and daughter. I know what Phoebe did."

Rebecca didn't know what to say. She couldn't quite grasp the implications of what Mary had just told her.

"Then I heard you and Phoebe talking," Mary continued. "And I understood. The colonel and I never had children, but if I had a daughter I would very much like to enjoy the relationship you clearly have with yours."

"I'm not sure what you mean," Rebecca took a sip of her tea and realised it had gone cold. "What are you going to do? Are you going to tell the police?"

A smile appeared on Mary's face. It was a warm smile that spread from her mouth to her eyes.

"Of course not," she said. "I think what Phoebe did was done with the very best of intentions and no matter the outcome, if the intentions are pure that's the most important thing."

A strange humming noise could be heard close by. It was followed soon afterwards by a flashing light on the wall above the kettle.

"My phone," Mary explained. "My sister in Seattle came up with the idea. I'm going to ignore it. I assume you received my gift."

"The book," Rebecca said. "I did, thank you. I must admit I was rather baffled."

"Read it," Mary said. "There are some very interesting chapters about the benefits of certain plants. They can be very beneficial in helping to keep unruly guests at bay. I couldn't help noticing some of those plants are already thriving in your garden. Others you can purchase at most garden centres."

Rebecca wasn't quite sure what this elderly American lady was suggesting, but she was starting to get a vague idea.

"Read the book," Mary said. "You'll see what I mean. And if you need any advice I'm always here."

"Thank you," Rebecca said. "I think. Shall we go next door? Henry will be wondering where we are."

"Today is your day, Rebecca," Mary said. "It's a day to push everything to the side. Everything can be kept for later when you try hard enough."

"I'm still concerned about the police," Rebecca admitted. "What if they find something."

"They won't. And if they had done they would have come calling by now."

* * *

Fifteen miles away in Bournemouth Detective Inspector Catherine Reece was experiencing mixed emotions. The results had come in from the post mortems of the three fatalities during the school reunion and DI Reece now had an exact cause of death for all three. All of them had suffered cardiac arrest. Acting on her initial suspicions the pathologist had performed tests to ascertain whether the dead guests had ingested some form of benzodiazepine at the reunion. Those tests came back positive. It was a result but it merely confirmed what DI Reece already knew deep down. And unfortunately, due to the fast-acting and relatively fast breakdown nature of Flunitrazepam there was no way to confirm if other guests had ingested the same drug. By the time the post mortem report came in too much time had passed.

Nevertheless, DI Reece remained positive. Something about the night of the reunion was definitely *off*. She could feel it and when that happened, she knew she wouldn't be able to rest until she had all the answers. And now the detectives inside the briefing room in Bournemouth were waiting for her to begin.

"Afternoon," she began. "Let's make a start. Last weekend a group of men and women attended a reunion for Grey Comprehensive in a cottage on Brightwater Lane in Frisk. Thirty-one people were there for the class of '89 party. Sometime during that reunion something happened that culminated in the deaths of three of the guests. All three died at roughly the same time and all three died from massive cardiac arrest. We've now confirmed traces of the drug commonly known as Rohypnol was found in their bloodstreams. What we now need to focus on is how it got there."

A young DC with a crewcut put up his hand.

"Go on, Robert," DI Reece said.

"Are we assuming these three people were murdered, Ma'am?"

DC Taylor had only recently joined the team. He was keen but he had a tendency to be too keen sometimes.

"Their deaths are suspicious," DI Reece said.

"Do we know if they're connected in any way?" DC Taylor added. "Besides being in the same class at school, I mean."

"Fredrick Fisher," DI Reece said. "Tom Stuart and Rachel Young. According to what we've managed to gather from friends and family none of the three have had any contact since school. Apparently they weren't that close even back then. I do not believe the link between the victims is important here."

"So, they're definitely victims?" A grey-haired man in an ill-fitting suit asked.

DS Jeff Hunter had been with Bournemouth CID for longer than anyone could remember. He was a couple of years away from retirement and his attitude reflected this. He did just what was expected of him and nothing more.

"Right now, I'm treating the deaths as suspicious," DI Reece said. "If it were a case of three individuals ingesting a drug and dying as a result of that drug it could be explained as a tragic episode but we have reason to believe they weren't the only ones at that reunion who ingested it. Nearly all of the people we spoke to had little if any recollection of the entire night, and I'm sure you're all aware that one of the side-effects of Rohypnol is memory loss."

"So somehow they all managed to take the drug?" It was DC Taylor. "How is that possible?"

"I think I've come up with an explanation for that," DI Reece said. "There were a few people at that reunion who didn't experience memory loss. Which leads me to conclude they didn't ingest the drug. Two of those people mentioned a bowl of punch that was there for anybody to dip into throughout the night. I believe that's the source of the Rohypnol. Most of the reunion guests drank some of that punch. Unfortunately, by the time this information was brought to light it was too late."

"The bowl was smashed to pieces," DS Lloyd Bright spoke for the first time. "Someone must have knocked it over and by the time we realised where the drug came from everything had been cleaned up."

"Do we have anything to go on?" DC Taylor asked.

"I believe we do," DI Reece replied. "But before I touch on that I want to run through the timeline for that evening. Some of the guests arrived on the Friday but the majority got there on Saturday afternoon. The party started and around five that afternoon it was interrupted by the residents of the cottage next door. One of the reunion guests remembered two women asking if they could turn down the music and move a car that was parked in front of number 10. The car was moved as requested."

"Did they turn the music down?" DC Taylor asked.

"We're not sure. Then sometime later one of the reunion guests remembered how everyone began acting strangely. People were falling over and being sick. Some people were unconscious outside. The guest we spoke to also told us he didn't drink any of the punch. Someone else who didn't touch the punch mentioned a woman who wasn't part of the reunion party and we later ascertained she was one of the women who came and asked the guests to turn the noise down. Phoebe Green – her parents have just moved in next door and she happens to be known to us."

"She was pulled with a sack full of roofies ten years ago," DS Bright elaborated. "She was let off with a slap on the wrists."

"Do you think this Phoebe Green is involved?" It was DC Taylor again. "Do you think it could be her who spiked the punch?"

"We've spoken to Miss Green," DI Reece said. "And she denied any involvement, and until we have something more concrete to go on, there's nothing we can link to her."

"Nobody we've spoken to remembers seeing her anywhere near that punch bowl," DS Bright said. "But it was her. I know it was her that spiked that punch."

"Where does that leave us?" DS Hunter asked. "As far as I can see we've got three stiffs who haven't seen each other in thirty years and we've got a whole load of witnesses with serious amnesia. We're not going to get any further in this investigation - I say we leave it at that."

"Excuse me," DI Reece said. "I must have heard wrong. Are you saying we ignore the fact three people are dead and their deaths are suspicious?"

"That's exactly what I'm saying, Cat. Sometimes you need to know when to back off and admit defeat."

"I see. Thank you for your insight, Jeff, but I cannot do that. Three people died at a reunion party last weekend and I'm going to find out why."

## CHAPTER THIRTY THREE

Henry inspected the meat on the grill and estimated it would be ready in about half-an-hour. He'd managed to escape Lionel King and now Colin was suffering a bombardment of anecdotes from Lionel's time in the Territorial Army. Lionel's wife, Diana was having a lie down in the living room.

The sound of music could be heard close by. Henry looked over the fence to the garden of number 12 but all was quiet there. The music got louder and Henry realised it was coming from the other side of Mary Major's house. He'd forgotten number 6 was also a HomeFromHome weekend rental.

Lionel came over and cast a disapproving glance at the meat on the grill. "Here we go. More out-of-towners who think they can do what they please."

"Sounds like they're staying next door to Mary," Henry said.

"We've been taken over," Lionel said. "Invaded. Diana and I have had enough."

"I couldn't help but notice the *For Sale* sign," Henry said.

"It's time to get out. You should think about doing the same."

"We've only just moved here," Henry reminded him.

"You'll see. My Diana used to be fit as a fiddle but now her nerves are shot. We're getting out before it's too late."

"I see the cottage is being listed with Needham Properties," Henry said.

"They seem to have places all over. We bought Sea View Cottage through them."

"I couldn't give a hoot who sells the place," Lionel said. "As long as we get shot. That meat smells like it's burnt."

The meat wasn't burnt. Henry flipped the chops and sausages over and gave Colin a knowing smile. The music from next door to Mary was still blaring and then suddenly everything went quiet. Shortly afterwards Mary and Rebecca emerged from the kitchen. They walked up to Henry.

"I won't ask," he said.
"Your wife is incredible," Mary said. "I have no idea what she just did but it seemed to work."
"Trade secret," Rebecca said. "How far is the meat?"
"Not long now." Henry told her.
"Susan and Phoebe have everything under control in the kitchen, mum," Colin said. "You are not lifting a finger today."
"I feel bad," Rebecca said. "It doesn't seem right sitting back and watching you all run around after me."
"Have you given any thought about what plants you're going to buy from the garden centre?" Henry asked.
"I've good a pretty good idea," Rebecca said and winked at Mary.

They ate outside in the garden. Katie and Paul made an appearance just as everything was ready. The twins had always had an uncanny knack for sniffing out a meal. Lionel King gobbled his food down in minutes and announced it was time for his wife's afternoon nap. He didn't even bother to thank Henry for inviting him.

"What an obnoxious man," Phoebe said.
"He's got his cottage up for sale," Henry said. "I saw the estate agent put up the sign earlier."
"Why are they moving?" Colin asked.
"Lionel reckons the guests are playing havoc with his wife's nerves. And you'll never guess who's selling the place? Needham Properties. The shifty giraffe-neck bloke was here himself."
"Good riddance to him, I say," Phoebe said. "He's a nasty piece of work if you ask me. At least you've got Mrs Major next door. She seems lovely."
"Your mother and her have been thick as thieves," Henry said. "I'm glad Rebecca has someone next door she shares things in common with."
"Where are they?" Colin said.

"Probably discussing how much that trip to the garden centre is going to set me back," Henry said. "When I wrote *the sky's the limit*, I did actually have a limit in mind."

"How much can a person actually spend at a garden centre?" Phoebe asked.

"I suppose I'll soon find out."

The afternoon turned into early evening and Mary said she needed to go and water her plants.

"Thank you for a wonderful afternoon," she said to Henry. "I'm so happy you and Rebecca moved next door. I may even consider putting my aids in more often."

"The guests at number 6 still haven't figured out what I did to their music," Rebecca said.

"Together we'll beat them," Mary gave Rebecca a hug. "You give some thought to what we spoke of earlier."

"What did she mean by that?" Henry asked Rebecca when Mary had gone.

"Just gardening stuff, love," Rebecca said. "She offered some advice about what plants I ought to buy."

"Well, I'm glad you've found someone to share your interests with. I was never the green-fingered type – it's nice for you to have a partner in crime."

"You don't know how right you are. I suppose I'd better make a start on clearing up."

"Everything's done, mum," Colin said. "Me and dad have already sorted it."

"You're spoiling me now. Although I think I could probably get used to it."

"Do you fancy a drink at the Frisk Arms?" Colin asked. "Me, Susan and Phoebe thought we'd take a walk down there and have a few drinks."

"What do you think, love?" Henry asked Rebecca.

"I think I'll stay here with Alfie," she said. "You go, though."

"Are you sure? It's your birthday."

"Go and have a few pints. Mary bought me a book for my birthday and I'm quite keen to start reading it."

"What book was that?" Henry said. "I didn't see it."

"Gardening stuff," Rebecca said. "Nothing you would be interested in."

## CHAPTER THIRTY FOUR

Rebecca had a strange dream that night. By the time Henry and the kids had returned from the pub she'd managed to read two-thirds of the book Mary had given her. The subject matter of the book wasn't what Rebecca would normally be interested in but in light of recent events she found herself glued to the pages. She never realised the dangers that lurked in the most innocent of places. She'd never have guessed that the beautiful foxgloves that grew at the bottom of the garden contained cardiac glycosides such as digitalis. Henry's favourite flower held the potential to cause vomiting diarrhoea, and in severe cases, cardiac arrest and death.

Rebecca was also unaware of the potentially lethal effect the nectar of the rhododendron could have on people with underlying heart problems. The neurotoxins present were known to cause severe symptoms in even the healthiest of people. The bark from the rhododendron could also cause problems in the functioning of the nerves, muscles and heart.

So it went on. By the time Henry, Colin, Phoebe and Susan arrived back from the Frisk Arms Rebecca was truly engrossed in the book.

And that was why when she awoke just before dawn the next morning and recalled snippets of the dream, she knew immediately the book: *Death by Stealth* was the inspiration.

Strawberries played an integral part in the dream. Ripe, juicy, red strawberries were everywhere. Some of them were blackened and others were oozing something white. There were no people in the dream – only fragments of green and brown existed beyond the strawberries and when Rebecca finally woke she remembered one scene very vividly. A leafy shrub grew larger before her eyes then sprouted berries that burst in front of her face. Jet-black berries exploded and sent a sweet-smelling vapour into the air. The fragrant spray turned foul – the stench was so pungent Rebecca could taste it even in dreamland. She found herself drifting into blackness and that was when she woke up.

A gap in the curtains allowed a shaft of light into the room. The sunlight sliced the bed in two. Alfred was asleep on Henry's legs at the bottom. Rebecca got out of bed and went to the bathroom. She smiled when she realised someone had left the toilet seat up. She knew it wasn't Henry – her husband had been trained in that respect a long time ago, and she guessed it had to be Colin or Paul. Rebecca had always loved having a house full of people. She enjoyed the chaos that went with it. Peace and quiet in a house with a sea view was all well and good, but Rebecca preferred to have people to share it with.

She made some tea, opened the back door and went out into the back garden. The strawberries were thriving next to the fence. Some of them would need picking soon. The ripe strawberries brought back pieces of a dream Rebecca could still make no sense of. She rarely dreamt these days and when she did the dream was usually forgotten almost immediately.

The sun was low over the Solent in the distance – it was still very early, and everything was silent. Rebecca went back inside and retrieved the book from the sideboard. She wasn't sure why, but she didn't want Henry to see what she was reading. *Poisons and Poisonings, Death by Stealth* was sure to arouse some suspicion on his part.

She opened the book and tried to remember the last page she'd read. She hadn't used a bookmark, so she flipped through the pages to try and jog her memory. As she skim-read the pages something on one of them jumped out at her. In the chapter about Animal and Vegetable toxins something was different. There were pencil marks on some of the pages. Someone had underlined parts of the text in black pencil. As she turned the pages she saw more pencil marks. She couldn't remember if they had been there when she first read the book, but she was sure they hadn't. It was very peculiar. She couldn't come up with an explanation – she'd hidden the book as soon as she'd opened the package and she'd put it straight back when she'd finished reading the previous evening. She wondered if the pencil marks had always been there. Perhaps she hadn't noticed them before. Yesterday had been a tiring day and she'd read the book inside the house. Perhaps the black pencil was more obvious now in the natural light outside. She wanted to see which parts had been underlined but she didn't get the chance.

"Morning, mum." It was Phoebe.

Rebecca put the book on the table, face down. "Morning, love. Kettle's not long boiled."

"My head hurts," Phoebe groaned. "That local brew is lethal."

"You've only yourself to blame. There's some painkillers in the cupboard above the kettle."

"Never again," Phoebe said and went inside, rubbing her temples.

The rest of the family didn't make an appearance for another two hours. Even Paul and Katie slept late. The twins came outside to the garden and for once, there wasn't a mobile phone or tablet in sight.

"Morning, you two," Rebecca said. "Do you want some breakfast?"

"Mum's making it," Katie told her and sat down next to Rebecca.

Paul walked over and before Rebecca could stop him, he picked up the book from the table.

"Cool. Katie, look at this."

He shoved the book in her face, so the cover was inches from her eyes.

"Urgh," she said and backed away.

"Kiss the frog, Katie," Paul said and moved the book closer.

"That's enough, you two," Rebecca took the book from Paul and slid it inside her dressing gown.

Colin and Susan came outside together. Both of them looked tired and hungover.

Colin sat down and groaned. "I think a fry-up is in order."

"How much did you lot have to drink last night?" Rebecca asked.

"Too much," Colin said.

"Where's your father?"

"He's just got up."

"He didn't drink that much," Susan said. "He only had a couple of pints."

"I wish I'd done the same," Colin said. "Does anyone feel like organising that fry-up?"

An hour later everyone seemed to be much more awake. Henry was just about finished drying the dishes when Rebecca came in the kitchen.

"It's a bit late to make the trip to Bournemouth now, don't you think?"

It was already half-ten in the morning.

"The kids all had a bit of a skin-full last night," Henry said. "I don't think they'll be in the mood for a drive."

"I suppose there'll be other times," Rebecca said. "We're not going anywhere. We can just enjoy a quiet Sunday here at the cottage."

"Why don't we invite the colonel's wife over for a late lunch?" Henry suggested. "We can have something to eat before the kids go back."

"That sounds like a wonderful idea," Rebecca agreed. "We don't have much in, though."

"I'll head out to Milford. There's a supermarket there and there'll be a bigger selection than here in Frisk."

Paul and Katie insisted on going with Henry to Milford. Henry was more than happy to oblige. Sea View Cottage seemed to have had a positive effect on the twins. They'd barely touched their phones since they'd arrived and even the PC in the study hadn't been used like it was back in Wimbledon.

They went out to the car and Henry spotted Lionel King across the road. He was smoking a cigarette next to a BMW. Henry hadn't even realised Lionel smoked.

Henry opened the car. "You two get in. I'm just going to say hello to Mr King."

He walked across the road and the first thing he noticed was the *For Sale* sign had been taken down.

"Morning," Henry said. "Have you had a change of heart?"

Lionel took a long drag on his cigarette and exhaled a huge cloud of smoke. "What?"

"The *For Sale* sign," Henry said. "I see it's gone."

"We've sold the cottage."

"That was quick."

"Apparently that's how these estate agents operate," Lionel said. "Mr Needham already had a client in mind when he listed the place - he brought someone round this morning and that was that. The buyer signed on the spot."

"Very convenient," Henry said. "I hope you got what you wanted for the place."

"Hardly. We didn't even get half what we paid for it, but I suppose beggars can't be choosers. If we don't get away from this hellhole, I don't think my Di will be able to take it any longer. The new owner is just having a last quick look around before he heads back to London. I left them to it. Do you know I haven't smoked a cigarette in ten years? I just had a craving for one while I was signing the papers."

"I don't blame you," Henry said.

The front door opened and two men appeared in the doorway. One of them was extremely tall with a neck that seemed even longer and thinner today.

"That's Mr Needham and the new owner," Lionel said.

Henry knew Darren Needham well by now. And when he registered who the *new owner* was he realised straight away that Lionel King had been well and truly taken to the cleaners. The man standing next to the giraffe-necked estate agent wasn't as tall as him but the family resemblance was quite apparent. Lionel had just sold his cottage to Darren's brother, Keith.

## CHAPTER THIRTY FIVE

Henry didn't mention the bizarre deal that had just been made across the road when he returned from Milford. Firstly, he didn't want to spoil the rest of the time he had before his family returned to London. The second reason he didn't broach the subject was he really had no idea what was going on. Why had Keith Needham bought Lionel King's cottage and why did Darren Needham neglect to mention to Lionel the potential buyer was his brother? Henry put it out of his mind.

He unpacked the groceries and switched on the kettle.

"Mary said she'd love to join us," Rebecca told him. "The kids aren't heading back until four so we can have a nice late-lunch in the garden."

"I'll make some tea. Have you seen the difference in the grandkids since they've been here?"

"Isn't it lovely? Katie and Paul have hardly touched their phones. And the PC hasn't even been switched on today. They're out in the garden picking strawberries."

"They'd better not eat too many," Henry said. "I bought enough food to feed an army."

"You know what the twins are like," Rebecca inspected a packet of ham. "They're always hungry."

Mary Major arrived just after one. The colonel's wife had brought a home-made apple pie with her.

"Never come empty-handed," she said to Rebecca in the kitchen. "That's what the colonel always used to say."

"That's not going to last long with my lot around," Rebecca told her.

"Have you had a chance to have a look at the book I bought you?"

"I started reading it last night when the kids went down to the pub," Rebecca told her. "I must admit it's very intriguing."

"Isn't it just? I have an identical copy. When I saw it on Amazon I couldn't resist and after speaking to you I just knew it was just the book for you."
"Why did you underline some of the words?"
The frown on Mary's face told Rebecca this was news to her.
"I didn't notice until this morning," Rebecca said. "I didn't realise you'd highlighted some parts by underlining them in pencil."
"I'm afraid I have no idea what you're talking about, Rebecca. What bits were underlined?"
"I didn't get the chance to look properly."
"That is very odd," Mary said.
"Perhaps someone did it before you bought the book," Rebecca suggested.
"I don't think so. That book was brand new. It was bought from Amazon, brand new and wrapped in plastic."

Colin came in and made a beeline straight for the apple pie. "I am definitely having a slice of that later. Afternoon, Mrs Major."
"Please, call me Mary," Mary said. "It's my special recipe. Us Yanks are proud of our apple pie heritage."
"Is there anything I can do?" Colin offered.
"Thanks, love," Rebecca said. "But we'll manage. You go and rest your sore head."
"I feel better after breakfast. I'll leave you to it."

"You really do have a lovely family," Mary said. "You and Henry must be very proud."
"We are," Rebecca agreed. "Our Phoebe went off the rails a few years ago but she's got her life back on track and she's doing well for herself. And our Col has always had his head screwed on. We should have known he'd become something like an accountant someday."
"There's goodness in all of you," Mary said. "All of you. You don't often see that these days."

Henry and Rebecca laid the food on the table outside. Henry had bought a selection of cheese and cold meats from Milford as well as spring rolls, samosas and chicken wings. Susan had made some sandwiches and now there was a spread fit for a king in front of them.

"Dig in," Rebecca said. "I don't want to see anything left."

Paul and Katie didn't have to be told twice. The twins were first to the table and soon both of them had plates stacked high.

"Save some room for Mary's apple pie, you two," Rebecca said.

"We will," the twins said in unison.

Everyone helped themselves and soon all that was left on the table were two chicken wings and half a tuna sandwich. Paul and Katie were lingering around the table.

"Go on then, you two," Rebecca said. "The chicken wings are yours."

"I'll wash up," Colin offered.

"You'll do no such thing," Rebecca said. "You're our guests, and guests do not do the dishes."

"You're spoiling him, mum," Phoebe said.

"Nonsense. Col, why don't you and your dad grab a few pints down the pub. Us girls will clear up."

"I've never heard such sexist bull in my life," Phoebe said. "What century are you living in, mum? The men go down the boozer while the women clean up after them?"

Mary smiled. "Listen to your mother, dear. Sometimes the old ways are the best."

Phoebe stared at her with her mouth open. "Are you serious?"

"I was brought up in an age where we took care of our men."

Phoebe shook her head.

"We washed their clothes," Mary continued. "We wore gloves, chopped them up and buried them in the garden. And when that was done we acted dreadfully sad at the funeral."

Phoebe looked at Mary for a split second then burst out laughing. It lasted for quite some time.

"I'm so glad my mum and dad moved next door to you," she said when she'd managed to control herself.

"I'll do that washing up then," Colin said.

"We'll do it," Phoebe was still chuckling. "I'm sure Mary will entertain us while we're busy."

"The guests in number 6 seemed to quieten down after I got into their Bluetooth," Rebecca said and placed the last plate on the draining rack. Rebecca, Phoebe and Mary were finishing off in the kitchen.

"They did," Mary said. "I didn't hear another peep out of them until this morning."

"Some people just don't know how to behave," Phoebe said.

"They need to be taught, that's all," Mary said. "Can you believe they had the nerve to ask if I had any sugar they could borrow?"

"Cheeky buggers," Phoebe said. "What did you say to them?"

"Nothing, dear," Mary said and winked. "I gave them a bowl of sugar."

## CHAPTER THIRTY SIX

"That is very interesting," Detective Inspector Reece said.

DI Reece was speaking to a colleague in Basingstoke. It had been almost two weeks since the reunion in Frisk and they were no closer to finding out exactly what happened than they were at the beginning. All three of the dead guests had been released – their bodies laid to rest and DI Reece had nothing more to go on. No more witnesses had come forward. None of the reunion guests had remembered anything else other than what they'd initially told DI Reece and her team, and DS Hunter's words were starting to ring true.

*Sometimes you need to know when to back off and admit defeat.*

DI Reece couldn't do that. It wasn't in her nature to back off and when something in an investigation didn't feel right it usually meant that it wasn't right. She knew instinctively there was more to the deaths of those three reunion guests than what everyone else could see on the surface. Unfortunately, time was running out and DI Reece knew it was only a matter of time before she was told to stop digging beneath the surface. Subtle hints were dropped then more, obvious ones, and it was clear that the incident at the HomeFromHome rental in Frisk was about to be swept under the carpet to join the rest of the hopeless cases that top brass thought were no longer worthy of investigation.

But now there was a glimmer of hope. DI Reece had worked under DI Jack Durham in Basingstoke and they still kept in touch on occasion, and what DI Durham was telling her now had piqued her interest.

"That is very interesting," she said once more. "I'll run it by the DCI but it's too much of a coincidence to ignore. Thanks for the tip-off."

"You think something is going on down there, don't you?"

"I'm sure of it," DI Reece said. "And I'm going to find out exactly what that something is."

She hung up and thought about what DI Durham had just told her. A young man had been rushed to hospital complaining of stomach cramps. He had a fever and was struggling to breathe. His condition deteriorated during the night and he died early the next morning. The doctors who treated him were baffled. None of them could form a diagnosis based on his symptoms. They'd never come across anything like it before. Tests were carried out but the exact cause of death was still unclear.

When one of the doctors learned the man's wife had also been feeling unwell his suspicions were aroused. The woman had complained about similar symptoms but hers were much milder and she'd made a full recovery.

Standard procedure in a sudden and unexplained death is to inform the police and Basingstoke CID became involved. DI Durham spoke in depth to the dead man's wife and something strange was brought to light. She and her husband both became ill at roughly the same time. And they weren't the only ones. Four of the couple's friends also came down with the same symptoms. All of them recovered after a few days.

What DI Reece found interesting was what the dead man's wife had told Basingstoke CID. All the people who displayed similar symptoms to the ones the dead man showed had something in common. They'd recently spent the weekend at a HomeFromHome rental in Frisk. They'd rented out number 6 Brightwater Lane.

Top brass couldn't turn a blind eye to this. The three dead reunion guests could be brushed under the carpet, but the death of another HomeFromHome guest was too much of a coincidence to ignore. DI Reece left her office and raced down the corridor.

* * *

"Have you seen what's just arrived next door?" Henry said.

He'd just returned from taking Alfred for a walk.

"More guests?" Rebecca guessed.

"They look like they came here in a time machine," Henry said. "Straight from the late-sixties. Hippies."

"That's not too bad then," Rebecca said. "At least they'll have decent taste in music."

"I hope so because they've brought their own instruments. Bongo drums, guitars and something that looked like bagpipes. And a digeridoo, if you can believe it. No amount of IT wizardry is going to put paid to what they have in store for us. There's two cars parked outside number 11 too."

"Mr Needham's?"

Henry had told her that Keith Needham had bought Lionel King's cottage earlier in the week. Neither of them could understand why he'd bought it and they also couldn't figure out why the place was sold so cheaply.

"I wonder if Keith Needham is using the cottage as a holiday home," Rebecca said.

"Neither of the cars was his," Henry said. "He drives one of those fancy BMWs. I wonder..."

The penny had dropped. "That bastard."

"Henry," Rebecca said. "Language."

"Sorry love," Henry said. "But that word is part of the English language and if I'm right it is a very appropriate informal noun under the circumstances."

"What are you going on about?"

"I'll let you know in a minute, but I'm sure I'm right."

He was. After a quick excursion across the road Henry returned with a furious expression on a very red face.

"The bastard."

"Are you going to tell me what's going on?" Rebecca asked him.

"I knew those Needhams couldn't be trusted. I spoke to a woman across the road. She's never heard of Keith Needham."

"What's she doing in his cottage then?"

"What do you think? Number 11 is now another HomeFromHome rental."

## CHAPTER THIRTY SEVEN

"Thank God for that," Henry exclaimed when the last of the cars that had been parked in the road pulled away from the kerb.

It had been an exhausting couple of days. Numbers 6, 12, 14 and 16 Brightwater Lane had been occupied by HomeFromHome guests all weekend. Keith Needham's newly-acquired cottage also had people staying and together they'd made the weekend so unpleasant Henry and Rebecca had been forced to leave their home for a while just to get some peace and quiet.

The hippies had booked all three cottages to the left of Sea View Cottage and Henry and Rebecca had been forced to endure dismal renditions of obscure sixties songs. Henry was certain he would hear the hum of the digeridoo in his ears for days to come. If that wasn't bad enough the guests across the road at number 11 clearly took umbrage to the music the free-love brigade was pumping out and turned their own music up to drown out the hippies.

"I'll put the kettle on," Henry said. "Roll on Sunday afternoon, that's going to be inscribed on my gravestone, I can tell you."

"We shouldn't have to put up with this, Henry," Rebecca said. "Something needs to be done."

"What? We've tried everything. You hacked their music, and they found a way around it. We've tried speaking to them, and look how that turned out. The police aren't interested and now we know HomeFromHome aren't either."

"I'm starting to see why Lionel King sold up and buggered off," Rebecca said.

"Let's not let it get us down, love. Let's enjoy the peace while it lasts. Tea?"

"No thanks," Rebecca said. "I'm just popping next door. I'll let the colonel's wife know it's safe to put her hearing aids back in."

Henry made his tea and was on his way out to the garden when he heard the sound of a car door slamming outside on the road.

"What now?"

Shortly afterwards the doorbell sounded. Henry put his teacup on the kitchen table and went to answer the door.

It was DI Reece and DS Bright.

"Good afternoon, Mr Green," DI Reece said.

"Afternoon," Henry said. "What can I do for you?"

"Can we have a word?" DS Bright asked.

"You'd better come in. Kettle's just boiled. Would you like something to drink?"

"Coffee would be great," DI Reece said. "If it's not too much trouble."

"Of course not. Make yourself comfortable in the living room and I'll bring it through."

He placed a tray of coffee, sugar and milk on the coffee table.

"What's this all about?"

"Is Mrs Green not home?" DI Reece asked.

"She's next door with Mrs Major," Henry told her. "Do you want me to go and get her?"

"That won't be necessary. How are you settling in? Moving can be such a headache."

"It's been quite painless, but you're not here to talk about the move, are you?"

"No," DI Reece said. "No, we're not. Have you had any more trouble with any of the HomeFromHome guests?"

"My head is still pounding from the last lot," Henry said. "They're a real nuisance. Mr King from across the road was forced to sell up because it was becoming detrimental to his wife's health. It's disgusting there's nothing we can do about it."

"I'm very sorry about that."

"Are you? Your lot couldn't care less. I paid my taxes for forty-odd years to help make this country what it is today and I'm starting to wonder if it was money wasted."

"We're getting side-tracked now." It was DS Bright.

"Then I suggest you say what you came here to say and leave me to enjoy what little peace I've got left of the weekend."

"Right," DI Reece said. "A week ago, there was an incident involving some guests at one of the HomeFromHome rentals."

"You mean two weeks ago," Henry corrected. "The reunion was a fortnight ago."

"No, this is something entirely different."

"What happened?"

"That's what we're trying to ascertain," DS Bright told him.

Henry started to laugh. He couldn't help it.

"Is something funny, Mr Green?" DS Bright asked.

Henry glanced at DS Bright's hand. He was wearing a wedding ring.

"Do you talk to your wife like that?"

"I'm not following you."

"*Ascertain* is a rather overused verb in detective circles, wouldn't you say? It's another detective cliché. Why don't you just say that's what we're trying to find out. Or establish, determine or verify? Why is it always *ascertain*?"

"What we're trying to *understand*, Mr Green," DI Reece interjected. "Is why a man who'd recently stayed at one of the HomeFromHome rentals ended up dead."

"I'm very sorry about that."

"He was twenty-seven years old," DI Reece continued. "He died on Wednesday."

Henry remained silent. He wasn't quite sure where DI Reece was heading with this information.

"Well, Mr Green," DS Bright said.

"Well, what?" Henry said. "DI Reece's statement didn't call for any comment on my part."

"The man who died rented number 6," DS Bright said.

"And?"

"And now he's dead," DI Reece added. "That's four guests from two separate rentals in the space of just over a week. Don't you think that's odd?"

"Yes," Henry said.

"Yes what?" It was DS Bright.

"Good Lord, man," Henry said. "What's wrong with you? Your boss asked if I considered it odd and I answered in the affirmative. Did you not sleep well last night?"

"Do you like strawberries, Mr Green?" DI Reece asked.

"I'm partial to a strawberry or two," Henry replied. "We have a nice strawberry patch in the back garden."

"That's interesting," DS Bright said.

"If you say so."

"The thing is this," DI Reece said. "We spoke to the widow of the man who died, and she mentioned something that caught my attention."

"Go on."

"When the guests arrived at number 6 on Friday evening, there was a bowl of strawberries waiting for them in the kitchen. Of course, the guests assumed it was a courtesy gift from the owner of the cottage, but when we asked the owner he knew nothing about it. Don't you think that's odd?"

"Yes," Henry said and glared at DS Bright.

DS Bright had the good sense to remain silent.

"All of the guests enjoyed the strawberries," DI Reece carried on. "And all of them became ill."

"The wife of the deceased told us her husband happened to eat more of the strawberries than the others," DS Bright said. "And that got us thinking."

"Glad to hear it," Henry said.

"What we're trying to find out," DI Reece said. "Is who left those strawberries there and why did the guests become ill from them."

"I've never been sick from eating strawberries," Henry said.

"Me neither," DI Reece said. "And at first that made me doubt whether the strawberries were actually related to the man's death, but then something else occurred to me. Whoever left the strawberries there didn't do it out of kindness – they didn't intend to welcome the guests, they wanted to deter them."

"Are you implying the strawberries were tainted in some way?"

"I am. The symptoms the dead man displayed before he died were very odd. Even the trained medical professionals looking after him were baffled. He suffered severe gastrointestinal discomfort and cardiac problems. His heart rate slowed to such an extent the muscles around the heart couldn't pump enough blood and his organs began to shut down one by one. It was a very painful death, Mr Green."

"Poor man," Henry said. "I'm still not sure how I can help you. I can assure you I didn't leave those strawberries in number 6 and I most certainly didn't poison them. What do I look like to you? The Wimbledon Poisoner?"

"We're just trying to eliminate all possibilities." It was DS Bright.

"You're trying to *discount* all possibilities," Henry corrected. "Where did you learn to speak English? Mongolia?"

"I think that's all for now, Mr Green," DI Reece said. "If there's something we've overlooked we will be back."

"I suppose that's better than saying *we may need to speak to you again,"* Henry said and turned to DS Bright. "You can learn a lot from your boss."

"We'll be on our way," DI Reece said. "We need to speak to the owners of numbers 4 and 8. You said your wife is next door?"

"That's right. You're wasting your time. You know that, don't you?"

"No, Mr Green," DI Reece looked him in the eye. "I don't believe I am."

## CHAPTER THIRTY EIGHT

Rebecca Green's mother always maintained there was good in everyone. Agnes Green was born four years before the start of the Second World War and when she returned to London after the evacuation, she'd experienced things no ten-year-old should ever have to go through. Hardship had made her see the world differently and as the post-war austerity faded and the world began to heal from the wounds of the war, the fifties was a time of hope and promise. Agnes looked to the future with optimism – she was able to look past the murky surface and find goodness in everyone she met.

Rebecca came into the world at the end of the 1950s – she was born into a time of change, and she too found the hidden depths many others couldn't see. The angry lollipop lady outside the school Rebecca's grandchildren attended was a good example. Psycho Sue was a fierce, hefty woman who instilled the fear of God in everyone, young and old, but Rebecca was able to look past the terrifying exterior and see something different in Psycho Sue. Here was a woman who had suffered terrible pain in her life and her gruff persona was simply a result of that suffering. It didn't take long for Rebecca and Psycho Sue to become friends.

No, Rebecca Green could always find goodness inside a person eventually.

Until now.

The thugs and hooligans enjoying a stag party at the HomeFromHome weekend rental next door were an exception to this rule. They'd announced their arrival at lunchtime with a car sound system that had shaken the foundations of Rebecca and Henry Green's cottage – it was now almost ten at night and the noise had increased to such a level Henry could no longer hear the television.

This couldn't go on - Rebecca had told Henry. This had to stop. Henry had always done his best to avoid confrontation and he'd argued they were only letting their hair down – blowing off a bit of steam. The *guests* were only a nuisance at weekends, he'd said.

But Rebecca wasn't going to put up with it anymore. And as the she gazed out onto the back garden and felt the vibration of the bass speakers on the window, an idea started to take shape in her head. It was late May, and the garden was in full bloom. The belladonna Rebecca had recently acquired had taken well to its new home and the pinkish-purple of the foxgloves had almost reached the top of the fence. It had been a close call the first time the police had come calling, but this time Rebecca decided they wouldn't have a clue what was happening. They wouldn't know where to start looking.

A booming voice from next door announced another round of drinking games was in order and at the same time an empty beer bottle was flung over the fence into Rebecca's prized rose bushes.

There was no good in these people, she decided. No good whatsoever. And it was high time someone put an end to the hell these HomeFromHome rentals were causing for the residents nearby.

* * *

"Are you out of your mind, woman?" Henry said.

Rebecca had told him about her idea. She'd explained it was a last resort, but they were running out of options.

"You can't just go around poisoning people," Henry added. "What's wrong with you?"

"This has to stop, Henry," Rebecca said. "It can't go on. We didn't spend our whole lives dreaming about a cottage by the sea only to have that dream shattered by a bunch of inconsiderate hooligans."

"There has to be something else we can do."

"What? We've tried reasoning with the guests, we've tried complaining to the police and HomeFromHome and look where that's got us. Listen to that racket. I'm not going to put up with it anymore."

The guests next door were screaming, and the sound of smashing bottles could be heard. Someone had brought along an air pistol and the pop of the gun could be heard at intervals.

"Poisoning the guests is not an option."

"What do you suggest we do, then, Henry Green?" Rebecca said. "If you've got a better idea I'd very much like to hear it."

"I don't know what to do," Henry admitted. "But I do know that poisoning people is not only immoral, it happens to be against the law. I don't fancy spending my retirement behind bars."

"That won't happen. It's been almost a month since the reunion. The police are still none the wiser. They won't know what's happening if we're careful. And look at the incident with the strawberries. They've got nothing."

Henry looked at his wife. There was genuine fear in his eyes.

"What do you know about the reunion guests? Do you know who left the strawberries at number 6?"

"Whoever was responsible for the deaths of the reunion guests got away with it, Henry," Rebecca said. "And I'm sure it was Mary who left the strawberries. She's got a lovely strawberry patch in her garden, and I think she poisoned them with something and left them for the guests at number 6. It's so bizarre and out of the box nobody would even consider it."

Henry rubbed his temples. "I can't believe you're even contemplating this."

"Look what happened after those people died, Henry. We had peace and quiet. Bookings were cancelled."

"That lasted all of five minutes. People still keep coming, love. There's nothing we can do about it."

"We just haven't put up enough resistance," Rebecca said. "I've hacked the sound systems but that doesn't stop them screaming and smashing things. Our Alfie is cowering under the bed right now. The poor bugger has a heart attack every time that air gun goes off. We need to take drastic action."

"Absolutely not," Henry said. "We are not poisoning the guests and that's the end of it. I don't put my foot down very often, but I am now. This topic of conversation is closed."

The pop of the air pistol was followed by an explosion of glass and a loud cheer. It was almost eleven and the guests next door were showing no sign of winding down the party. Rebecca took a few deep breaths and went to the bedroom to check on Alfred.

## CHAPTER THIRTY NINE

When Henry woke the next morning the cottage was quiet. Rebecca wasn't in the bed next to him. He dressed and went through to the kitchen. He turned on the kettle and opened the back door to let Alfred out. There was a note on the kitchen table. Henry picked it up and started to read. It was from Rebecca.

*Mary and I are taking a walk to the Sunday market. I'll pick up something nice to eat.*

"Hmm," Henry said.

He couldn't remember the last time Rebecca had left him a note. His wife was a list-maker, not a note-writer. Alfred came back inside.

"She's up to something," Henry told the Jack Russell. "That woman is up to something."

He took his tea outside, walked up to the fence and surveyed the carnage left by the guests next door. There were bottles everywhere. Most of them were smashed to pieces and there was broken glass all over the lawn and flower beds.

The current guests were all men – they were attending a stag party and things had got out of hand. Just before midnight Henry and Rebecca were woken by an almighty din. Two of the men had got into a fight and a verbal slanging match soon escalated into a physical attack. The fight lasted for quite some time and when Henry looked out of the window he'd watched at least half-a-dozen men try to break it up. He wondered if there would be a few walking wounded at the wedding.

An hour passed and Rebecca still hadn't returned. Some of the stag party guests were stirring. Henry could hear moans and groans coming from next door and he smiled. He hoped the hungover men would be out of action for a while. He glanced at the foxgloves at the end of the garden and something caught his eye. Henry didn't know much about gardening, but he did know enough to recognise a weed when he saw one. He got up from his chair and walked down the path that split the small stretch of lawn in two.

His eyes hadn't deceived him. In amongst the glorious pinkish-purple of the foxgloves was another, much smaller plant. Its flowers were also purple, but these were much darker in colour. The leaves too were darker green and more spread out than the foxglove's tight foliage. The purple, bell-shaped flowers were attractive to look at, but Henry thought the black berries had a sinister aspect to them. Lurking inside shells of green there was something malevolent in these berries. Some of the berries had fallen away from their stalks onto the soil below. Henry debated whether to rip up the entire plant by its roots but decided not to. He was no expert, and this could be one of the plants Rebecca bought from the garden centre for all he knew. He left the mysterious plant alone and went back to his tea.

It was the Sunday of the Spring Bank Holiday and Mary Major had told them this was when the tourist season started in earnest. The colonel's wife had warned them about the busier roads and the strangers who invaded the small village at this time of year. Henry wondered if the HomeFromHomes would become more bearable. Surely the calibre of guests would improve and the weekend rentals would be families with children and not the city louts they'd had to put up with for the last month.

Two of the stag party men were outside now. Besides the occasional groan they were rather subdued. One of the men stood next to the fence, rubbed his eyes and nodded at Henry. He didn't look well at all. His hair was unbrushed, his skin was deathly pale and there were dark rings around his eyes. There was a bruise the size of a pound coin on his left cheek.

Henry remembered his own stag party as being rather uneventful. A couple of close friends at a local pub was about as much as he dared. He couldn't see the point of getting married with a thick head and he really didn't see the attraction of getting rat-arsed with a bunch of other men the day before you said *I do* to the woman you were about to spend the rest of your life with. Of course, things had changed since then. Stag nights somehow escalated to stag weekends and often whole weeks were spent binge drinking before the big day. Henry doubted if the groom next door was about to tie the knot anytime soon. No, things had definitely changed since Henry and Rebecca were married.

There was one thing that would never change, however. A hangover would always be a hangover and in Henry's limited experience on the subject the only cure is to let time do its thing. The splitting headaches and fragile stomachs of the men next door would pass in time.

"Morning, mate," the man next to the fence shouted to Henry.

Henry found himself nodding to him.

"You don't have any aspirin, do you?"

"I'm afraid not," Henry replied.

The other man appeared next to him. "I don't suppose you have any miracle hangover cures?"

"Don't drink so much the night before," Henry offered.

"Very funny. My head feels like it's been hit with a train."

"I may have something that will help," Henry said.

"Anything," the man groaned. "Anything at all."

"Hold on."

Henry went inside the house and suddenly wondered what on earth he was doing. Why was he feeling so charitable all of a sudden? He reasoned it was because he was young once too. OK, it had been a very long time ago, but he must have been the same age as the men next door at some stage in his life, and their pleas for help had stirred up something inside. These men who, not long ago were beating the living daylights out of one another seemed vulnerable somehow. And Henry couldn't bear to see it.

"Drink this."

He handed each man a glass filled with a dark brown liquid.

"What is it?" the bruised man asked.

"An old family recipe," Henry said. "Water, raw eggs, sugar, salt and a secret ingredient I'm afraid I can't divulge. It tastes a bit bitter, but I promise you this will sort you out."

The bruised man took a tentative sip and winced. His friend did the same.

"It tastes bad," Henry said. "But it does the job. Try and get it all down."

"Does it really work?"

"It'll either cure you or kill you, as my old nan used to say. Come on, get it down your necks."

"What's going on?" It was Rebecca.

Henry hadn't realised she'd come home.

"Morning, love," Henry said. "I was just helping these lads with their thick heads."

Rebecca turned around and went inside.

"Thanks, mate," the man with the bruise handed the empty glass back to Henry. "I think I feel better already."

"I hope it does work," his friend said. "We've got quite a bit planned for the do later. Neil is going to be in no state to get married when I've finished with him."

He too handed Henry his empty glass.

"What was that all about?" Rebecca said in the kitchen.

There were a few plastic bags on the table.

"Come on, love," Henry said. "We were young once."

"We knew how to behave ourselves. Those lot are hooligans and you're encouraging them."

"They were suffering. I couldn't bear to see it so I gave them something to make them feel better. Have a heart, love."

"I don't understand you sometimes."

"What's in the bags?"

"You're going to kill me," Rebecca said.

Henry smiled. When Rebecca said this it meant one thing, and one thing only – she'd spent money on something she didn't really need. More often than not it was something she bought on a whim and something that never saw the light of day again.

"What have you bought this time?" Henry asked.

"Don't kill me now," Rebecca said and started unpacking the bags.

She pulled out a two plastic boxes. Inside each one was some kind of leather case.

"For the twins' tablets," Rebecca explained. "You know how our Col is always moaning about them dropping them? These are supposed to protect them. They were half the price you pay in the shops."

"I'll make some tea," Henry said ten minutes later.

Rebecca had finished unpacking the bags and now the kitchen table was covered in her purchases – most of them destined to see out their days in the back of a cupboard. Henry didn't care. Rebecca seemed to have forgotten about his fraternising with the enemy next door and all was well with the world.

# CHAPTER FORTY

They heard the sirens of the ambulance an hour later. Henry was finishing off the Sunday crossword and Rebecca was considering where to display the trinkets she'd bought from the market. Henry got up and walked over to the window. The sirens were getting louder. A group of men were standing outside on the road. Most of them had mobile phones glued to their ears.

"What's happening?" Rebecca asked.

"I have no idea," Henry said. "But that ambulance sounds like it's getting closer."

It pulled up outside number 12 a couple of minutes later. Two paramedics got out, and were instantly pounced upon by some of the stag party guests.

"Something's happened," Henry stated the obvious.

"Perhaps one of them has come down with alcohol poisoning," Rebecca said. "It'll serve them right. Bunch of yobos."

Henry looked at her. "You didn't..."

"I didn't what?"

"What have you done, Rebecca?"

"I haven't done anything."

"Why is there an ambulance parked outside number 12?" Henry said. "You haven't gone and poisoned the guests, have you?"

"I really have no idea what you're talking about, Henry. Whatever the reason for that ambulance, it has nothing to do with me."

Henry carried on watching. The scene outside had gained momentum and more people were now on the road. A crowd of men and women Henry didn't recognise had joined the stag party men – more HomeFromHome guests, Henry assumed and now the road outside Sea View Cottage resembled Wimbledon on match day.

The paramedics went inside the cottage and appeared a few minutes later with a man on a stretcher. After putting him in the ambulance they went back inside the house and another man was brought out.

"I'm going to see what's going on," Henry said and headed for the front door.

Rebecca followed him out. A police car had now arrived and two officers in uniform were speaking to some of the stag party guests. Henry walked over to them.

"What's happened?"

"We're not sure," the taller of the two PCs replied. "Are you part of the stag party?"

"Not likely," Henry said. "We live in the cottage next door."

"Ah yes," the other PC looked Henry up and down.

"What's that supposed to mean?"

"There's nothing to see here. Could you please go back inside? I imagine someone will be round to speak to you during the course of the day."

"Right," Henry said to Rebecca in the kitchen. "Something's going on. I didn't very much like the tone of that PC's voice. When he found out I lived next door he started acting strange."

"Do you think that woman DI has said something?" Rebecca asked.

"They think we're involved, love," Henry said. "And the way they were acting leads me to believe we've got another couple of deceased HomeFromHome guests."

"If that's the case, that's six in the space of a few weeks."

"I don't trust that DI Reece," Henry carried on. "She's a wily one and I get the impression her dogged determination won't let her stop until she gets to the bottom of things."

"Do you think she's going to pay us another visit?"

"I'm not a gambling man," Henry said. "But I'd put money on it."

"I really had nothing to do with this, Henry," Rebecca said.

"I know, love. I know you didn't and I apologise for even suggesting it. Let's just carry on, regardless and when those detectives do come knocking they're going to go away disappointed. We've done nothing wrong, so we've got nothing to worry about."

* * *

The knock on the door came later that afternoon. All was quiet next door and the majority of the guests had left. The stag party weekend was over and the only sound from next door was the occasional clink of a bottle as the forensic team from Bournemouth went over the scene with a fine-toothed comb.

Something was different about DI Catherine Reece when Henry opened the door. He sensed it straight away – she nodded to him and smiled and Henry knew immediately something was wrong. DI Reece knew something. DS Bright was standing behind her.

"Can I help you?" he asked.

"Lloyd," DI Reece said to DS Bright.

The middle-aged detective sergeant took a few sheets of paper out of his jacket pocket.

"We're getting to be like old friends," Henry said. "We'll be exchanging Christmas cards before long."

"I'm afraid this isn't a social visit, Mr Green," DI Reece took the sheets of paper from DS Bright and showed it to him. "This is a warrant to search your property."

"This has to be some kind of joke," Rebecca had appeared in the doorway.

"The suspicious deaths of six people is no laughing matter, Mrs Green." It was DS Bright.

"Six?" Henry said. "So, the two stag party guests didn't make it then?"

"They were dead before they got to the hospital," DI Reece told him. "You are well within your rights to contact a legal representative but the search of your property will go ahead whether you do so or not."

"This is ridiculous," Henry said. "On what grounds did you even obtain a warrant to search our cottage?"

"We are under no obligation to answer that question," DI Reece said and handed Henry the sheets of paper. "That is a copy of the warrant as well as the codes of practice. Those are yours to keep."

"Don't you have to give us some kind of warning?" Rebecca asked. "You can't just barge in here and tear our home apart."

"I believed advance notice would have hindered the purpose of the search," DI Reece explained. "And I outlined as much in my application to the court. Under UK law you are entitled to be present during the search but if in any way I believe you to be obstructing the forensics officers I am authorised to force you to leave at any time. Do you understand what I've told you?"

"I'm not an idiot," Rebecca said.

"I apologise if I may have come across as patronising, but I am obliged to outline the procedure in as plain a language as possible. May we come inside?"

"It doesn't look like we've got much choice, does it?" Henry said.

"No, Mr Green," DS Bright said. "You don't."

## CHAPTER FORTY ONE

The forensics officers from Bournemouth didn't even acknowledge Henry and Rebecca when they came inside Sea View Cottage. Two men and a woman got to work in absolute silence. DI Reece and DS Bright suggested Henry and Rebecca wait outside in the garden. Alfred came out with them. The Jack Russell clearly wasn't happy about having his home invaded by a bunch of strangers.

"I won't offer you anything to drink," Rebecca said. "If it's alright with you."

"It would be better if you didn't touch anything inside for the time being," DI Reece said.

"How long is this going to take?" Henry asked.

"As long as it takes."

"I suppose you're not going to tell us what it is you're looking for?"

"I think you already know the answer to that question, Mr Green."

"It's going to rain later," DS Bright said. "Forecast reckons it's going to chuck it down all over the south until Tuesday. Typical Bank Holiday Monday weather."

Henry looked at him but didn't say anything. He wasn't in the mood to discuss the weather.

"Have you had any news about how the man who stayed at number 6 died?" he asked instead.

"We have," DI Reece said. "Mr Knight, his wife and four other guests somehow ingested a toxin that made them very ill. Unfortunately, Mr Knight had an underlying heart problem and that coupled with the fact he had more of the grayanotoxins in his system resulted in his death."

"Where did the poison come from?" Rebecca asked.

"That's what we're busy working on at the moment," DS Bright said.

"You think you're going to find the poison in there?" Henry pointed to the back door.

"We have to cover every angle," DI Reece said. "You see, these particular toxins are not something you see every day and there are very few places where the grayanotoxins exist."

"I can tell you now, they certainly don't exist inside our cottage," Henry said.

"No, Mr Green. They don't. But that toxin is present in your garden. In the flowers of the rhododendrons growing there."

"Excuse me?"

"Those flowers..."

The sound of breaking glass cut short what DI Reece was about to say next. It was followed soon afterwards by some choice words from one of the forensics officers.

"I've had enough of this," Rebecca said to DI Reece. "I'm not going to wait out here while your lot demolish our cottage."

The source of the noise was a salad bowl Rebecca and Henry had been given as a wedding present over forty years ago. A red-faced man had found a dustpan and brush and was busy cleaning up the mess when Rebecca went inside.

"I'm very sorry, Mrs Green," DI Reece said. "Bournemouth CID will reimburse you for the cost of a new one of course."

"You can't buy those anymore," Henry told her. "That bowl is over forty years old. This is outrageous."

"I'm phoning our Col," Rebecca said. "Not only are we being treated like common criminals, your lot are hell bent on smashing the place up."

She picked up her mobile phone and went back outside to the back garden.

"Would it be possible to speed things up a bit?" DI Reece asked one of the forensic team.

"We're doing our best, Ma'am," the woman said. "But we're not exactly sure what we're looking for."

"You're not going to find anything," Henry assured her. "And I'd appreciate it if you leave us in peace to enjoy what's left of the Sunday afternoon."

He went outside to join his wife.

"Colin is on his way down," Rebecca told him. "He's going to get hold of a lawyer and he advised us not to speak to the police until we've had some legal advice."

"Are they really allowed to do this?" Henry asked. "What gives them the right to barge in and harass an old couple like us?"

"Apparently they can. And the courts don't issue warrants without strong grounds for doing so."

"Sounds like they're in the main bedroom," Rebecca said. "God help them if they break anything in there."

"I just wish they'd give us a clue about what exactly it is they're hoping to find."

Something in Rebecca's peripheral vision caused her to look round. Mary Major was standing by the fence. Rebecca went over to speak to her.

"The police are searching our home," she said.

"So, I believe," Mary said.

"Have they been to speak to you?"

Mary tapped her ears. "I took my aids out as soon as I heard the knock on the door and played dumb."

"Two more men died. Two people at the stag do next door. Bournemouth CID think Henry and I know something about it."

"Let them think that," Mary said. "What are they going to find?"

"Nothing, I hope. I have no idea how those men died. The first I knew about it was when the ambulance pulled up outside. I still don't know what the police know that they aren't telling us. Our Colin is going to get in touch with a lawyer and he's going to come down as soon as he can."

"What did you do with the book?" Mary asked.

Rebecca froze. She found herself shivering in the afternoon sunshine. She'd forgotten all about the book.

*Poisons and Poisonings – Death by Stealth.*

It was hidden away in the sideboard, but when Rebecca thought about it, she realised it wasn't a very good hiding place after all.

"Good Lord," she said and remembered what DI Reece had spoken of. Grayanotoxins can be found in the nectar of the rhododendron flower and Rebecca recalled that was one of the sections of the book that had been underlined.

"I have to go," she said and rushed inside the cottage without offering any explanation.

"Almost done," DI Reece told her.

All three forensics officers were now working in the living room. The two men were crouched down next to the TV unit and the woman was making her way towards the sideboard next to the window. Rebecca could feel the throb of her heartbeat in her ears and her eyes were drawn to the door of the sideboard.

"Are you alright, Mrs Green?" DI Reece asked.

Rebecca nodded - her eyes focused on the sideboard the whole time.

"You look a bit pale," DI Reece added. "Are you sure you're alright?"

She followed Rebecca's gaze and her eyes came to rest on the sideboard. She glanced at Rebecca and walked over to the old oak sideboard. She took out a pair of gloves, slid them on and opened the door.

"I've already checked in there, Ma'am," the female forensic officer said.

DI Reece ignored her. She reached inside and retrieved one of the files Rebecca kept in there.

"I keep all our personal records on file," Rebecca told her. "Technology is all well and good, but it doesn't hurt to have a backup on paper."

DI Reece took out another file and Rebecca could feel her face heating up. She was starting to feel sick.

DI Reece opened the file, leafed through a few pages of bank statements and insurance correspondence then closed it again. She took a closer look inside the sideboard and replaced the two files. Rebecca opened her mouth and took a deep breath. There was nothing else inside.

The book she'd hidden there was gone.

## CHAPTER FORTY TWO

DI Reece and her team had left by the time Colin arrived later that afternoon. The shrewd detective inspector hadn't found anything incriminating inside Sea View Cottage – she'd admitted defeat but she'd assured Rebecca and Henry she would be back. Rebecca was still baffled by the disappearance of the book Mary had given her for her birthday. She tried to recall when last she'd seen the book – she was sure it was when the twins were playing with it outside in the garden, and she was equally positive she'd put it back in the sideboard when she had the chance. She remembered stuffing it inside her dressing gown and putting it back behind the personal files.

But now it had disappeared, and Rebecca didn't have a clue what had happened to it.

"Sorry to drag you into all of this, son," Henry said to Colin. "Do you want something to drink?"

"A beer would be great, dad," Colin said. "I told Susan I'd be staying the night so I don't have to drive back. What exactly happened here today?"

"I'll get you that beer," Rebecca said.

"There was a stag do next door," Henry told Colin. "Usual nonsense, although this lot were even more rowdy than the others. Shooting bottles with an air gun, they were."

"That's terrible."

"They were much quieter today and when the ambulance pulled up your mother and I knew something had happened. Two of the blokes were taken to hospital and they both died on the way."

"Good God," Colin exclaimed. "And the Bournemouth CID think you and mum had something to do with it?"

"They implied as much. But they were more interested in the man who stayed at number 6 the weekend of your mother's birthday."

"I read something about it."

"He had heart problems, you see and the police think he died because he was poisoned. They discovered some toxin that's not particularly common. It occurs naturally in the rhododendron. That's what the police were looking for, I think. That woman DI obviously noticed your mother's plants and put two and two together."

"And came up with three. They tore the cottage apart and besides breaking the salad bowl they achieved nothing." Rebecca had returned with the drinks.

Colin opened his beer and took a long sip from the bottle. "Thanks, mum. I needed that. You might have grounds for harassment. I spoke to a lawyer friend and from what I told him he thinks this DI Reece is bang out of order. My mate couldn't believe she managed to get hold of a search warrant based on what she has on you. He's offered to help if you want him to."

"How much is that going to cost?" Henry asked.

"Not as much as you stand to gain if you win."

"We don't want the stress of a big legal fight, Col," Rebecca said. "Not at our age. We left London to slow down a bit."

"Your mother's right, son," Henry agreed. "Those court cases have a habit of dragging on and on and we don't want that at our age. I just want them to stop bothering us."

"As if the guests are not enough," Rebecca said. "Now we've got the local police breathing down our necks."

"At least let my friend do something about that," Colin said. "He can do a bit of digging and find out exactly what Bournemouth CID think they have on you. It seems to me the evidence they do have is pretty flimsy and if that's the case he can make sure that this DI Reece thinks very hard before coming here and hassling you in the future."

"I suppose it won't do any harm," Henry said. "We just want to be left in peace to enjoy our retirement."

"Have you seen the state those forensic officers left the place in," Rebecca said. "They didn't even have the decency to put things back in the correct places. It's going to take me ages to sort the kitchen out."

Henry shook his head. There were jars of herbs and pickles left out on the worktop. Some of the jars had been left open and the lids were strewn all over the place. The dishes that had been stacked on the draining board were now covered in some kind of powder and would need to be washed again, and the black bin bag had been left open on the floor next to the fridge.

"Let's go out," Colin suggested. "Let's grab a bite to eat at the Frisk Arms. It'll do you both good to get away from the cottage for a bit, and we can make a start on cleaning up the mess some other time."

"I think that sounds like a really good idea, son," Henry agreed. "A few hours to forget about everything that's gone on sounds just what the doctor ordered."

It was starting to spit with rain so they drove to the pub. It was only a ten-minute walk but none of them felt like getting wet. As they drove Rebecca's thoughts turned once again to the missing book. She couldn't for the life of her figure out what had happened to it. The more she thought about it the more convinced she was that she'd put it back in the sideboard. She remembered the book outside on the patio table. Paul had picked it up and remarked on the frog on the cover and then he'd teased his sister with it. Rebecca recalled she'd taken it off him and hidden it inside her dressing gown. When the coast was clear she clearly remembers putting it back behind the files in the sideboard.

But now it had disappeared and wherever it had ended up – its new hiding place had been overlooked by the forensics officers from Bournemouth. It really was baffling. Mary Major had given her the book for her birthday, Rebecca had read some of it and hidden it away. Then the next time she picked it up someone had underlined certain sections in pencil. And now it was gone. Rebecca realised there was only one explanation – somehow Henry had discovered the book, realised its significance in light of the recent deaths and hidden it where the police would never think of looking, but the more Rebecca pondered this explanation the more ridiculous it seemed. Henry didn't have it in him. In the forty-odd years Rebecca had known her husband had never once broken the law. He hadn't so much as had a parking ticket or speeding fine in all that time.

Rebecca knew she wouldn't be able to rest until she found out what had happened to that book.

## CHAPTER FORTY THREE

The Frisk Arms was busier than they'd expected it to be. The rain was now falling quite steadily outside the window and the temperature had dropped. Rebecca and Henry sat down at a table while Colin went to get some drinks from the bar.

"Are you alright, love?" Henry asked. "You seem a bit out of sorts."

"I'm just a bit rattled by the police earlier," Rebecca said. "We've never had the police search the house before."

"They won't be back. Don't listen to a word that DI said – they won't be back."

"Who won't be back?" Colin had returned with the drinks.

He placed a glass of wine and two pints of Cat's Whiskers on the table.

"I was just telling your mother the police won't be back," Henry told him. "That DI Reece is going to be left with egg on her face if she keeps on badgering us."

Colin took a long drink of the beer. "About that. The police don't spend that much time and resources on nothing."

"What exactly is it you're implying?" Henry asked.

"It's just a bit odd. My mate said they must have had reasonable grounds to search the cottage otherwise a magistrate never would have authorised it."

"The police make mistakes too, Col," Rebecca said. "They're only human. And I'd quite like to talk about something else, if you don't mind. That was an experience I'd very much like to forget about."

They ordered three fish and chips and were told there would be quite a wait. The pub was packed, and the kitchen had a backlog of orders. Rebecca didn't particularly care – she wasn't very hungry, and the warm buzz of the red wine was making her feel much more relaxed. The whereabouts of the book was still niggling away at her and she wanted to try and forget all about it for a few hours.

"Katie and Paul have started karate," Colin said. "They've never really shown much interest in sports and Susan and I thought the discipline would do them good. They're loving it so far."

"Karate?" Henry said. "I'd better be careful with them from now on."

"Anything that gets them away from their phones for an hour or two is fine by me," Colin said. "There's a new club opened up just down the road, and a few of their friends are doing it too. It's doing them the world of good."

The food arrived and everyone tucked in. Rebecca ate with a gusto that surprised her. She hadn't realised how hungry she actually was. The three glasses of wine and the talk of family had put all thoughts of police searches and missing books out of her mind. This was just what she needed.

A familiar face walked through the door when they were halfway through the meal. Mary Major shook her umbrella in the foyer of the pub and hung it on the rack next to the door. The colonel's wife was wearing a long raincoat – she took it off and hung it next to the umbrella. She spotted the Greens and walked over to their table.

"Did you walk here?" Rebecca asked her.

"There's nothing like a walk in the rain to help wash away the woes of the day," Mary said. "You should try it."

"Come and join us," Rebecca said.

"I wouldn't want to impose while you're eating."

"Nonsense," Colin told her. "We're almost finished. Can I get you something to drink?"

"A scotch would go down very well," Mary said. "No ice and a little water, thank you. A double if it's not too much trouble."

"No trouble at all," Colin said.

He finished what was left on his plate and walked over to the bar.

Mary sat down next to Rebecca. "The police came back. There's something fishy going on."

"Was it DI Reece?" Henry asked.

"She's a stubborn one, that one. She asked all sorts of questions."

"What kind of questions?" Rebecca said.

"About how well I know you. What kind of people you are. Of course, I painted you in a good light. What else could I do?"

"That woman doesn't give up," Henry said.

"I get the impression she's under a lot of pressure," Mary said. "Six dead guests is quite a lot to get one's head around, wouldn't you think?"

Colin put the drinks on the table. Mary downed half the scotch in one go. She coughed. "That hit the spot, thank you. The colonel used to drink a dram every night after supper. No more, no less and he always maintained it was what kept the doctor at bay."

"How did you two meet?" Colin asked her.

Mary smiled and closed her eyes. "Long Island, 1958. I was nineteen-years-old. My aunt had a house in Stony Brook. We used to go there in the summer. The place wasn't grand like the ones you see in the Hamptons, but it looked right out onto Smithtown Bay. It was a glorious summer that year and my sister and I spent the whole of the vacation by the sea."

Colin noted her empty glass. "Would you like another one?"

"I suppose one more isn't going to kill me," Mary said. "Where was I?"

"Long Island, 1958," Henry reminded her.

"Ah, yes. There was a big party for the July 4th celebrations, over in Northport. I wasn't a big fan of those things back then and I was ready to leave when I spotted him. He was one of those men who made everything around him disappear if you know what I mean. William seemed to have the ability to make everyone else fade into the background. He caught me staring and he came over. I was shy in those days – I was only nineteen, but William was the easiest man to talk to and we talked, I can tell you that. The sun went down and when it rose the next day we were still talking. Time didn't seem to exist."

She looked down and noticed Colin had returned with her drink. She hadn't even realised he'd come back.

"It turned out William was on a weekend R&R from Fort Wadsworth in the city," she continued. "He was twenty years older than me but that didn't matter. He shone like no man had ever shone before and that was it – I was his if he wanted me. And he did. He told me that night that he'd dedicated twenty years of his life to the army and now he was ready to dedicate the rest of it to me. We were married soon after in the fall."

"What a wonderful story," Rebecca said.

"Isn't it just," Henry agreed.

"William saw out his time at Wadsworth," Mary said. "He was stationed out west for a while and after a tour in Vietnam we left the army life behind us. We arrived in England in 1970. William would have been a hundred-years-old this year. Oh my, that makes me feel terribly old."

"Nonsense," Henry said. "You're wise, not old."

Mary placed her hand on his. "The colonel would have liked you, Henry. I believe he would have liked you very much."

"What was he like?" Colin asked. "Besides being an army colonel – what was he like?"

"Determined," Mary replied. "He refused to let anything get in his way. He had hopes and dreams and he told me just before he died, he'd fulfilled all of those dreams. He used to say that if a dream is meant to be realised, it will be."

"I like that," Rebecca said.

"The colonel was a practical man," Mary added. "But he was also a dreamer and I soon realised that the combination of those traits made him an unbreakable force. When we have dreams we ought not to let anything get in the way of them."

"I'll drink to that," Rebecca said. "Nothing should be allowed to get in the way of a dream."

## CHAPTER FORTY FOUR

Rebecca and Henry never imagined they'd be heading back to London so soon after moving to Frisk, but the following week they found themselves heading north up the M3 towards the city they'd spent most of their lives in. Colin had suggested they get away from the cottage for a weekend. Their first month in Frisk hadn't exactly been what they'd expected. The six dead HomeFromHome guests and the constant visits from Bournemouth CID had been rather traumatic and Colin had proposed some time away. Henry and Rebecca had been reluctant at first – they'd both refused to be forced to leave their dream retirement cottage, but in the end, Colin had persuaded them it would do them some good to get away. And as they packed the car for the weekend and heard the boom-boom of the stereos in the car belonging to the latest round of HomeFromHome guests both Rebecca and Henry had decided it was probably a good idea.

Colin had also twisted his mother's arm further by reminding her the garden centre close to where he and his family lived was considerably better stocked than the one in Milford. Rebecca hadn't been able to get everything she wanted from Milford and there were still quite a few plants and shrubs she hadn't ticked off her list. They would be able to kill two birds with one stone – they could get away from the cottage for a while and pick up the plants at the same time.

Henry was making sure Alfred would be comfortable in the back of the car when the red Audi stopped outside number 12. The four young men and women who got out were clearly not fazed about what had happened there the week before. The deaths of two of the stag party guests seemed to have little effect on them. Two of the women and one of the men were obviously already quite intoxicated already even though it was not yet two in the afternoon. The driver of the Audi seemed to be the only sober one. They retrieved their luggage and went inside number 12 without even acknowledging Henry. Shorty afterwards the familiar sound of the offensive speakers inside the cottage could be heard.

"That's that then," Henry said to Rebecca. "Alfie's sorted. Is there anything we've forgotten?"

"I don't think so," Rebecca replied. "And we're only going for the weekend."

"I'll just go and make sure the doors are locked. We don't want to take any chances what with that rabble next door."

He walked up the path to the front door. The music got louder as he walked. He unlocked the front door and went to see if they'd remembered to lock the back door. One of the windows in the kitchen was open so he closed it. As he was about head back to the car, he heard an ungodly noise from next door.

"Here's Penny!"

He looked out of the window and caught a glimpse of a half-naked woman parading around in the garden. Dressed only in her bra and knickers the suggestive dance she was performing wouldn't have been out of place in a Soho pole-dancing club. Henry averted his eyes, closed the front door and locked it. He was suddenly glad to be getting away for the weekend.

Henry had decided to get in touch with DI Reece to inform her they would be in London for the weekend. Rebecca had wondered why he'd bothered but Henry had told her it was for the best.

"If anything happens to any of the guests this weekend," he'd said. "That Bournemouth detective inspector needs to know we were nowhere near the place."

Henry had been surprised at DI Keene's reaction when he'd phoned. She seemed appreciative and she actually apologised for any upset the visits from CID may have caused.

Colin and Susan owned a house just outside Richmond. The three-bedroomed property was situated close to the campus of the University of Roehampton and Richmond Park. Colin had fallen in love with the area ten years ago – it was far enough from the city to forget about the hustle and bustle, yet it was close enough for the daily commute into the heart of London.

Henry pulled up outside and turned off the engine. The drive from Frisk had been rather uneventful – the early Friday afternoon traffic had been kind and they'd made it to Richmond in just under two hours.

"I'll grab His Lordship out the back," Henry said. "And take him across the road to the park so he can stretch his legs."

He attached the lead to the Jack Russell's collar and coaxed him out of the car. Alfred arched his back and sat on the pavement staring up at Henry. Henry gave a slight tug on the lead. "Come on, you. Let's see if you need to empty that bladder of yours."

They went across the road and walked a few metres inside the park. Henry took out his mobile phone and Rebecca watched as he held the phone to his ear. Alfie sniffed the grass, lifted his leg and urinated against a fence post.

The door to Colin and Susan's house opened and Susan stepped outside. Katie and Paul came out and ran up to Henry's car. The twins gave Rebecca a reluctant hug.

"We have to help you with your bags," Paul said.

"That's very kind of you," Rebecca said. "They're in the boot. We didn't bring much."

Henry walked back across the road. "His Lordship has done his thing. Hello, you two."

"Hello granddad," the twins said at the same time.

"What's this I hear about you two playing judo," Henry said.

"It's karate, granddad," Katie said and let out a long sigh.

"It's totally different to judo," her brother added. "Mum said we have to carry your bags."

"It'll be good for your muscles," Henry said. "If you're going to do karate properly, you're going to need strong muscles."

This seemed to do the trick. The twins soon made short work of taking the luggage out of the boot and lugging it to the house.

"Colin won't be long," Susan told Rebecca and Henry inside. "He's just having a few drinks with a client, and he'll be home soon. Tea?"

"That would be lovely," Rebecca said. "I'll give you a hand."

She and Henry followed Susan into the kitchen.

"Who were you talking to on the phone?" Rebecca asked Henry.

"Nobody," Henry said.

"I saw you on the phone."

"Oh, that. Someone left a voicemail the other day and it slipped my mind. It was someone offering gardening services. They must have heard we've moved into Sea View Cottage and thought they'd try their luck."

"I'm not having anyone messing around with my garden," Rebecca said.

"That's what I thought. Speaking of which, did you bring that list of plants you still need to get?"

"Of course. I know exactly what I still need for the garden."

Henry sighed. "I'm going to regret telling you the sky's the limit, aren't I?"

"You can't go back on a promise, Henry Green."

"I appreciate that," Henry said. "But when I said the sky's the limit I meant the sky over Milford, not the entire stratosphere of planet earth."

Susan poured the tea. "Have you heard anything more from those detectives?"

"Not a sausage," Henry said. "I think they've figured out they're barking up the wrong tree and they've moved on to some other line of enquiry."

"Colin thinks you should sue for harassment."

"It's not worth the bother, love," Rebecca said. "We just want to be left in peace."

"Bournemouth CID have just misunderstood the whole situation," Henry added. "People make mistakes all the time, even the police."

"Well, at least if anything does happen this weekend at one of those HomeFromHome places," Susan said. "There's no way they can suspect it had anything to do with someone eighty miles away."

## CHAPTER FORTY FIVE

If Henry and Rebecca were in Frisk that weekend, they would have thought it impossible for four people to make so much noise. The din coming from inside number 12 Brightwater Lane was unbelievable. It was starting to get dark and the two couples were now so drunk none of them were actually paying any attention to what the others were saying anymore.

Next door Sea View Cottage was dark and silent and across the road Lionel King's old cottage was also in darkness. The only HomeFromHome occupied was number 12, but what the guests lacked in numbers they were making up for in volume.

A loud shriek from number 12 drowned out the sound of a window being broken next door. The intruder nudged the broken glass aside with his elbow and reached inside, trying to locate the lock next to the kitchen door. He flipped it open, went inside the kitchen and closed the door behind him. He waited a moment for his eyes to adjust to the darkness then made his way to the counter on the other side of the room. Broken glass crunched underfoot as he walked.

Another scream from next door caused the intruder to stop in his tracks and take stock of the situation. He'd counted four guests – two men and two women. All of them were drunk and he doubted whether any of them would be in any state to put up much resistance.

He looked at the knife block and, after weighing up a number of options he decided on a carving knife with a heavy blade and a sturdy handle. Berghuis – an expensive knife set Henry had bought Rebecca for her sixtieth birthday. It felt reassuring in his grip. He looked outside into the garden. Darkness had fallen quickly, and the heavy clouds were obscuring the moon.

He decided to wait. There was no rush and he liked being inside Sea View Cottage. It felt warm and safe. Nobody would be coming here tonight, and he had all the time in the world. A half-full bottle of red wine on the table caught his eye and he decided to treat himself to a drink. A few sips wouldn't hurt. He raised the bottle to his lips and winced at the bitterness of it. A few more slugs and he could feel his heartbeat slow. He needed to relax a bit and the wine was doing him good.

A couple of hours later the only sound that pierced the silence was the occasional hoot of a nearby owl. The intruder finished what was left in the wine bottle, threw it in the bin and picked up the envelope on the table. He stuffed it inside his pocket without counting what was inside. It was far too late to worry about that. He left the same way he'd come in and made his way through the garden to the fence that separated Sea View Cottage from number 12. The fence was low and easy enough to hop over. A stray branch from a rose bush snagged on his jacket as he went. He yanked it away and wriggled free and there was a soft thud as something landed on the soil beneath. He paid no attention to it. His focus was on the task at hand.

He took three steps forward then stopped when he was overcome by a sudden dizziness. After a few deep breaths he carried on. His mouth felt very dry and his sense of smell was playing tricks on him. He was sure he could smell onions nearby.

The back door of number 12 had been left wide open and a single light had been left on inside the house. The intruder went in and banged his shoulder on the doorframe. He was having trouble keeping his balance. He regretted drinking the wine now – it was probably a bad idea.

There were three bedrooms inside the cottage. The first one, a very small room that contained just a single bed was empty. Two people were asleep in the second bedroom along the corridor. Fighting the waves of nausea that were coming and going the intruder finished what he needed to do and staggered towards the bedroom at the end.

In here were two more people. The curtains had been left open and as the clouds moved away from the moon the light caught the blade of the knife. But something wasn't right. The blood was white. And the metallic tang of it had been replaced with something more pungent, like garlic.

The intruder knew something was happening to him when he'd finished with the man and woman in the main bedroom. He couldn't just feel it – he could taste it. Like the bitterness of an aspirin swallowed without water it started on his tongue, moved down his throat and spread to his stomach. His breathing became more erratic, and sweat was starting to soak through his clothes. His throat closed up as he fought for breath. He could feel the skin on his face warming up and then a flash bomb exploded inside his head. The knife fell to the floor and he collapsed on top of the dead couple on the bed.

## CHAPTER FORTY SIX

The Peacock seemed different somehow. The pub around the corner from Henry and Rebecca's old house had been a haunt of Henry's for over two decades but now it didn't feel the same. Henry didn't believe for one second it could have changed so much in such a short space of time so he figured it was he who had changed and not his old local pub.

Colin had suggested a few drinks at The Peacock while Susan and Rebecca were at the garden centre and Henry hadn't argued. Garden centres weren't his thing and he could catch up with what had been happening in the area over a few beers. It was early Saturday afternoon and the pub was relatively busy. The patrons here were a mixed bunch. There were the locals who'd been coming for years – the odd passer-by who just happened to fancy a quick drink on the way to somewhere else, and, more recently the families and children. The landlord of The Peacock had kept with the times and now the old pub had a fairly decent menu to choose from.

"Cheers," Colin said. "Good to be back?"

"I don't know, son," Henry said. "I really don't know. It feels quite strange to be honest. It feels like I'm back prematurely. I never expected to return to London so soon."

"You'll always come back to London. Once London is in your blood there's no escaping it. Do you know if there are any guests next door this weekend?"

"They arrived just as we were leaving," Henry told him. "They were already drunk when they got there so Lord knows what they got up to last night. I caught one of them dancing half-naked in the garden. At two in the afternoon to boot. Some women have no shame."

"Lucky you," Colin said. "I bet there's a few old codgers in here who would pay to have that next door."

"Well, I didn't. Your mother and I bought that cottage for peace and quiet. And I'm buggered if I'm not going to get it."

"Perhaps they'll close the HomeFromHomes down," Colin said. "Perhaps they'll close them if more people die in them."

"Six people are dead already, son, and it hasn't made a blind bit of difference. Besides, I doubt anyone will be murdered this weekend, what with me and your mother out of the picture."

"I still can't believe they thought you had something to do with it," Colin said. "It's actually quite surreal. Although *the poison pensioners* does have a certain ring to it."

"The whole debacle has been a damn nuisance. God knows what they teach the police in training school these days. They're incompetent, the whole lot of them."

Henry frowned when he spotted a familiar face. Arnold Havisham had spotted him too and Henry's old neighbour was heading straight for their table.

"Alright, Henry," he said. "What brings you back? Got fed up of the quiet, did you?"

"Arnold," Henry said. "Rebecca needed some things for the garden, so we just popped back to pick them up."

"Settling in alright, are you?"

"Very nicely, thank you."

"I heard about the dead guests," Arnold said. "Terrible business. I read about it in the papers. Was that anywhere near you?"

"Not really."

"We was thinking of coming down and paying you a visit," Arnold said. "But my Zo is too scared what with the dead guests and all."

*Glad to hear it,* Henry thought.

"Another pint?" Colin said.

Henry looked at his watch. "I imagine your mother will still be busy at the garden centre. I'll have the same again, thanks."

"Very civil of you," Arnold joined in. "Mine's a Stella."

Colin walked off to the bar leaving his father with Arnold Havisham.

"Do you know what happened?" Arnold asked.

"I'm afraid you're going to have to give me more to go on than that," Henry said.

"With the dead guests. The old bill aren't giving much away as usual and the papers aren't either. They reckon it could be something to do with the water down there. You ought to be careful. You could be next."

With this he started to laugh. Henry hadn't missed Arnold Havisham's grunt of a laugh one little bit.

Colin put the drinks on the table.

Arnold drained half his glass without a word of thanks. "I was just telling your old man he needs to watch the water down there where he's gone. Word is those guests died because they drank the water there."

"I don't think it had anything to do with the water, Arnold," Colin said.

"That's what they reckon in the papers. Those HomeFromHomes must be taking a bit of a knock."

"Not as far as I'm aware."

"I heard that lanky Needham geezer crying about it in here last night."

Henry's ears pricked up. "Darren Needham?"

"Dodgy eyes, that one. Him and his brother was in here with some other geezer. Zoe and me was on the next table so it wasn't like I was prying."

"What were they talking about?" Henry asked.

"The HomeFromHome rentals. Seems like they've taken a dip since this business with the dead guests. I promise you, it's the water down there. How else would you explain it?"

"Why would the Needhams be so concerned about the HomeFromHomes?" Colin said.

"I didn't catch all of it," Arnold drained what was left in his glass. "But it seems those brothers are in for a lot of dough in these weekend rentals."

"I'm not quite following you," Henry said.

"And here was me thinking you was an English teacher. From what I could gather I got the impression those Needham brothers don't just dabble in estate agency stuff – they own a load of those HomeFromHome rentals."

## CHAPTER FORTY SEVEN

"He was right," Colin said.

They'd just finished eating and he and the family were sitting in the living room waiting for Escape to the Country to start on the television. Colin had his laptop on his lap.

"The number on half the HomeFromHomes on Brightwater Lane is Darren Needham's," Colin added.

"And his brother bought number 11," Henry remembered. "Lionel King's place."

"Which ones does Darren own?" Susan asked.

Colin looked at the screen. "According to the website he's got number's 6, 12, 14, 16 and 19."

Henry stood up. "I don't know much about number 19 but that lanky bastard owns all the rentals that have been making our lives a living hell for the past month."

"And he still sold us Sea View Cottage," Rebecca said. "What exactly is he playing at?"

"Something untoward," Henry said and headed for the kitchen.

"Where are you going?" Rebecca asked him.

"I spied a bottle of whiskey in there earlier. I need something strong right now. You don't mind, do you, Col?"

"Of course not, dad."

Henry came back with the bottle and four glasses. He poured himself a generous measure and asked if anyone else cared for one. Nobody did.

"What is that giraffe-necked rat up to?" Henry said and sat down. "What is his agenda?"

"Perhaps it's an investment," Colin said. "Property is always a sound investment."

"No," Henry took a sip of whiskey and winced. "He's bought five properties on the same street. How on earth could he even afford them?"

It was as he was pouring his second glass that the penny dropped. He remembered something Lionel King had told him as he stood, dejected outside the cottage Keith Needham had just purchased. Lionel had seemed devastated. Smoking a cigarette for the first time in ten years, he'd mentioned something to Henry.

"He's planning on turning the whole street into a playground for drunken louts and whores."

"Henry Green," Rebecca said. "I think you've had enough of that whiskey."

"Lionel King got half of what he paid for his cottage," Henry said. "He told me so. He was so desperate to get out he'd take anything. I believe those Needhams are practically encouraging their guests to make as much noise as possible to they can get the properties for a steal."

"I'm inclined to agree with mum, dad," Colin said. "I think that scotch has gone straight to your head. That's a preposterous idea."

"Is it?" Henry realised he was shouting. "Is it? They make life hell for the neighbours then snap up the cottages when the owners are at their wits end. I'll wager what's left in this bottle that somewhere along the line your mother and I will be offered a pittance for Sea View Cottage."

"Let's all calm down," Susan suggested. "Escape to the Country is about to start."

Henry snorted. "Escape to the Country. Escape to the bloody Country? What sort of a programme is that?"

* * *

"It's a bloodbath in there, Ma'am."

DI Catherine Reece had been called away from a meal out with her husband. A surprise birthday party had been arranged at number 12 Brightwater Lane and the guest of honour had called the police after making a gruesome discovery inside the cottage. Four of her friends and a mystery man were dead inside. The PC who'd just spoken to DI Reece now sat on the wall outside with his head in his hands.

"A bloodbath," he repeated.

DI Reece got into a SOC suit and put on a pair of gloves. She breathed in deeply and made her way towards the front door of the cottage. A middle-aged PC was manning the door.

He nodded to DI Reece. "Ma'am. It's not a pretty sight in there."

"A forensics team is on the way," she told him. "I want the whole area sealed, front and back. I want tape around the whole property. And nobody is to come anywhere near the place."

"Understood, Ma'am."

DI Reece had a dreadful feeling of déjà vu. She'd been called out to Brightwater Lane far too many times in the past few weeks and she couldn't work out exactly what was happening here. Six people had died in this small, peaceful village in less than a month, and from what she'd been told when she answered the phone call, they now had five more dead bodies to deal with.

She smelled it as soon as she entered the cottage. It was an unmistakable stench and one that any police officer who has been at the scene of a brutal murder will never forget. The metallic tang of blood lingers in the nose and throat for quite some time.

She looked around and took everything in. The first thing she registered was there didn't seem to be anything to indicate any kind of struggle took place inside the cottage. Everything seemed to be neat and tidy – there were no overturned chairs or broken glass, and DI Reece came to the conclusion the victims were caught unawares. The back door was wide open and there was a light on inside the kitchen. She made her way down the corridor and looked inside one of the bedrooms. The bed was made and there was nobody inside the room.

A man and a woman were on the bed in the second bedroom. Both of them were on their backs and both of them were drenched in blood. More blood had soaked into the white sheets on the bed. When DI Reece took a closer look she realised the man and woman had both had their throats sliced open. The blood on their necks was dry and black.

The scene in the main bedroom was rather confusing. Another man and woman lay side by side on the bed and this couple too had had their throats cut. But there was another man in the room. Lying face down on top of the man and woman, his presence there was all wrong. DI Reece didn't want to touch anything until the forensics team was finished but her curiosity was aroused and she needed to try and put together a picture of what could have happened here. She took hold of the man's hair and gently lifted his head. His face was dotted with dried blood, but DI Reece couldn't find any obvious injuries. His eyes were open and a swollen tongue stuck out of a blue mouth. There was a carving knife on the carpet next to the bed. The blade was also covered in dry, black blood.

DI Reece went outside to the back garden and looked over the fence into the garden belonging to Henry and Rebecca Green. Sea View Cottage was still – there seemed to be nobody at home. The window in the kitchen was open - DI Reece remembered the phone call Henry Green had made to inform her he and his wife would be away for the weekend, and something stirred inside her. Why had he phoned to tell her this? It seemed like a very strange thing to do.

Something caught DI Reece's eye. There was something wrong next door. She took a closer look and realised what it was. The kitchen window wasn't open, there was no longer any glass in it. Someone had broken the window.

# CHAPTER FORTY EIGHT

"Someone broke into the cottage."

Henry had just got off the phone with DI Reece.

"You're kidding?" Colin said.

"Looks like they got in through the kitchen window," Henry added.

"Do they know if anything was taken?" Rebecca asked.

"DI Reece was rather vague. She just said the window in the kitchen was broken and she suggested we come home right away."

"You're hardly in any fit state to drive, dad," Colin said. "You've knocked back the best part of a bottle of whiskey.  And mum doesn't have a driving license."

"I'll drive Henry's car," Susan offered. "And you can follow in the people carrier. We can stay the night and come back in the morning. It's Sunday tomorrow anyway."

"The twins can stay with the Jones next door," Colin added.

"Thank you," Henry said. "I'd appreciate that."

"I hope they haven't taken anything," Rebecca said.

* * *

Two hours later they parked outside Sea View Cottage. It was starting to get dark, and the wind had picked up. A police cordon had been set up around number 10 and 12. Strips of tape had come loose and were blowing in the breeze. Two police cars and an ambulance were parked outside on the road as well as a number of other cars.

"That's a bit over the top for a housebreaking," Colin observed.

"And what's the ambulance doing here?" Susan asked.

"Let's go and find out," Henry said and got out of the car.

The phone call from DI Reece sobered him up in an instant but now the after-effects of the whiskey were kicking in. His head was throbbing, and his mouth felt extremely dry. He needed some water inside him.

DI Reece intercepted the Green family before they even reached the gate. The expression on her face told a story of its own.

"What's going on?" Rebecca asked.

"I'm afraid you can't go in yet," DI Reece told her.

"Why not?" It was Henry. "It's our house. Why can't we go inside?"

"Why is there an ambulance here?" Colin said.

"Something happened next door," DI Reece said. "At number 12. And the forensics team is still busy in there as well as inside Sea View Cottage."

"You told me the cottage had been broken into," Henry said. "What exactly is going on here?"

"I'm afraid I can't tell you at this stage. Have you been in London since yesterday?"

"We left just after I called you," Henry said. "And we drove straight here after you told me someone had broken into the cottage. Why can't we go inside our property? We need to see what's been taken."

"It doesn't appear to be a normal burglary. The kitchen window was broken and that's how we believe the intruder gained access but as far as I can tell nothing has been taken."

"Why would someone break in and not take anything?" Susan asked her.

"I really don't know what happened yet," DI Reece said. "All I know is what I've already told you."

"I don't believe you," Henry said. "The police do not send out this many officers for a break-in. A forensics team and a detective inspector do not attend the scene of a routine burglary. I want to know what's going on."

Before DI Reece could reply DS Bright approached. The middle-aged detective sergeant looked very red in the face.

"Lloyd," DI Reece said. "Have they found anything?"

"Can I have a word?" DS Bright said.

They walked off and Henry watched them talking. DI Reece listened to what DS Bright had to say and glanced back at Henry. They spoke for another few minutes and walked back over to the Greens.

"They're finished inside Sea View Cottage," DS Bright said. "There was nothing to find. Looks like the intruder smashed the kitchen window, opened the door from the outside and left the same way. There doesn't appear to be anything missing. The laptop is still there and usually that's the first thing they swipe. It's a really odd one, especially considering what happened next door."

"What happened next door?" Henry wasn't giving up.

DI Reece sighed. "OK. You're going to find out sooner or later. We got a call from a woman who was booked to stay in the HomeFromHome next door to you. It was supposed to be a surprise birthday party but when the woman arrived, she found four of her friends dead inside number 12."

"Five," DS Bright corrected. "There were five dead bodies."

"Four of her friends," DI Reece said once more. "The fifth victim was a complete stranger – the birthday girl had never met him before."

"I need some tea," Henry said.

DI Reece had told them they were allowed to go inside the cottage. It was now almost ten and the team from Bournemouth CID were still busy next door. Colin had cleaned up the broken glass from the kitchen window and taped a piece of cardboard over the gap left behind. There was fingerprint powder on the window frame and the door but besides that and the broken window it was as if nothing had happened.

"I'm going outside for some fresh air," Rebecca said.

"It's blowing a gale out there," Henry said. "You'll catch your death."

"I'll put my coat on," Rebecca said.

She opened the back door and went outside to the garden. Colin and Susan followed her out.

Henry looked around the room. Everything seemed to be in its place. He left the kitchen and had a look in all the rooms. Nothing had been disturbed in any of them. He stopped by the small desk in the study, took out the key and unlocked the drawer. He took out what he needed and returned to the kitchen. Shortly afterwards the doorbell rang.

It was DI Reece. She was standing on the doorstep with DS Bright. "What now?" Henry said. "Nothing appears to have been taken, so I don't know how we can help you."

"Could we come inside, Mr Green?" DI Reece asked him.

"You might as well."

He stood to the side and the two Bournemouth detectives walked past him. They headed straight for the kitchen. Henry closed the door and followed them.

DS Bright had a frown on his face when Henry came inside the kitchen. "Are you alright?" Henry asked him. "You look somewhat perplexed."

"I know what I saw," DS Bright whispered to DI Reece.

"Is there something I can help you with?" Henry said.

"We're sorry for disturbing you, Mr Green," DI Reece said. "There seems to have been some kind of misunderstanding. We won't keep you any longer. We'll see ourselves out."

She and DS Bright left Henry alone in the room. DI Reece glanced back as she walked. She stared at the block of knives on the kitchen counter. Berghuis – very expensive. Henry followed her gaze. The black-handled knives were all there. The sharp, carving knife was where it always was, next to the serrated bread knife.

## CHAPTER FORTY NINE

"You're a million miles off the mark, Catherine," DCI Jacob Gunn told DI Reece.

She was inside his office discussing the way forward prior to the Monday morning briefing. The team from Bournemouth had worked tirelessly since the brutal murders of four of the guests in number 12 Brightwater Lane and DI Reece was outlining her suspicions in light of what they'd found in the main bedroom of the cottage as well as what she'd unearthed in Rebecca Green's garden. It had been two weeks since the guests attending the surprise birthday party had been slaughtered and DI Reece's team were exhausted and extremely demoralised.

"This has nothing to do with a sixty-three-year-old woman," DI Gunn continued. "The very idea is preposterous."

"Just hear me out, sir," DI Reece said. "The first three victims had traces of Rohypnol in their systems. Rebecca Green's daughter was arrested for possession and intent to supply the stuff."

"And I believe we have nothing that links the drugs to Mrs Green?" DCI Gunn reminded her.

"It was her. The man who died at number 8 showed symptoms of some kind of poisoning. I did a bit of digging and the symptoms were exactly those systematic of the ingestion of the nectar from the rhododendron plant. Rebecca Green has the very same flowers in her garden. Not to mention the strawberries that I'm positive were covered in the toxin. There is a thriving strawberry patch in Rebecca's garden."

"You're barking up the wrong tree, Catherine."

"I'm not," DI Reece realised she'd raised her voice. "The other guests got sick, but they recovered. The man had an underlying heart condition and that's why he died. The strawberries were nothing to do with the owner of number 8, so what were they doing there? I'm positive Mrs Green left them there to poison the guests."

"Once again," DCI Gunn said. "There is nothing to link Mrs Green to the death of that man."

"Both men from the stag party died of the same thing, sir," DI Reece hadn't quite finished yet. "And, after a closer look in Rebecca Green's garden I have a strong suspicion about what killed them. Are you familiar with deadly nightshade?"

"Of course. The very name doesn't leave much to the imagination."

"Those men were poisoned, sir."

"Cause of death was cardiac arrest," DCI Gunn reminded her.

"Come on," DI Reece said. "What are the odds on two friends succumbing to a heart attack at the same time? Rebecca Green has deadly nightshade in her garden. The woman seems to have a fondness for lethal plants. There is a whole host of toxic flora in that garden. I'm going to focus on that aspect at the briefing. And I've brought in an expert to explain it in more detail."

"Expert?" This was clearly news to DCI Gunn.

"A woman from Southampton University. She's just completed a thesis in Phytotoxicology and she's one of the leading experts in the field of poisonous plants."

"Who authorised this?"

"I did, sir. Fran Munch knows more about toxins in plants than anyone else in the country – and she's not charging a fee."

"That's something at least."

"I'm onto something here, sir," DI Reece said. "Please, just humour me."

"OK," DCI Gunn said. "Let's say these HomeFromHome guests were poisoned – what's the motivation here? Why? And what about the four men and women who were murdered two weeks ago? They all had their throats

sliced open. And where does the mystery man found in the main bedroom fit into all this?"
"I don't know," DI Reece admitted. "The Greens were in London at the time of the murders but that got me thinking too."
DCI Gunn let out a loud sigh. "Go on."
"Henry Green called me to inform me he and his wife were heading up to London for the weekend. Why would he do that?"
"Out of common courtesy," DCI Gunn suggested. "In case we needed to contact him with regards to the recent deaths."
"Or to put him and his wife in the clear."
"Are you now suggesting Mr and Mrs Green were involved in the deaths of those four guests?"
"I don't know. Something about his contacting me seemed odd somehow. And the knife found inside number 12 was the same brand as the ones the Greens had in their kitchen."
"But the knives belonging to the Greens were all accounted for I believe."
"I don't know how to explain that."
"Until you do," DCI Gunn said. "I suggest you focus on what you can explain."
"That's what I plan on doing," DI Reece said. "But first I need to make a quick phone call."

* * *

Henry Green looked out from the patio at the sea in the distance. The early-morning sun was low in the sky but it was promising to be a glorious day. Henry felt content. It had been two weeks since the brutal murders next door and the HomeFromHome cottages had stood empty for the past two weekends. Rebecca had checked the website and all the bookings at the cottages belonging to Darren and Keith Needham had been cancelled. The press had given the murders a lot of coverage and the negative reports seemed to have had a detrimental impact on the weekend rentals. Henry couldn't have been happier. For the past two weeks he and Rebecca had been able to relax and enjoy the very reason they moved to Sea View Cottage in the first place.

The name seemed to have stuck, and Henry had no desire to change it. Sea View Cottage was very appropriate. The only sound to be heard on Brightwater Lane was the chatter of birds and the occasional car passing by.

Rebecca came outside with Alfred in tow. Even the Jack Russell seemed happier these days. Rebecca put two mugs of tea on the table.

"Thanks, love," Henry said. "Do you hear that?"

"What?" Rebecca said.

"Silence. Isn't it a sublime sound?"

The silence didn't last long. The sound of Henry's mobile phone ringing sounded louder somehow.

He went inside to see who it was.

"Mr Green."

Henry recognised DI Reece's voice immediately.

"That's right," he said.

"Is now a convenient time to talk?"

"I've got nothing else on the agenda right now."

"How much do you know about gardening, Mr Green?"

Henry didn't reply straight away.

"Mr Green?" DI Reece said. "Are you still there?"

"I'm still here. Gardening, you say?"

"I couldn't help noticing the thriving garden you have there at Sea View Cottage. It really is beautiful.

"Thank you," Henry said. "But I'm afraid you'll have to ask my wife about that. I know about as much about plants as I know about the breeding habits of the duck-billed platypus."

"That's what I thought," DI Reece said. "Sorry to bother you."

"No problem at all."

Henry came back outside to the garden.

"Who was on the phone?" Rebecca asked.

"Some salesman," Henry said. "Wanted to know if I was interested in timeshare down in Bournemouth. I told him I most certainly wasn't. Those foxgloves are creeping over the fence."

Rebecca glanced at the purple flowers. "I had debated whether to cut them back, but I decided I like them like that. They make the garden look wild somehow."

"They do," Henry agreed. "Do you feel like a drive to the sea?"

"I think I'll just potter in the garden for a while. Mary gave me some cuttings I need to plant. We can go to the sea another day."

"We've got years ahead to take trips to the sea," Henry said. "The sea is not going anywhere and neither are we."

"We've earned this, Henry Green."

"We have, haven't we, love?" Henry agreed.

## CHAPTER FIFTY

DI Catherine Reece looked at the faces in front of her and realised the sunken eyes and dejected expressions mirrored exactly how she was feeling right now. It had been over a month and a half since the three reunion guests had died – there had been eight more dead bodies in Brightwater Lane since then and they were no closer to finding out what happened there than they were right at the beginning.

DI Reece was seated at the table in the briefing room. A short, thin woman in her mid-thirties was sitting next to her. Dr Fran Munch had short, blond hair and her deep tan suggested she spent a lot of time outside the UK. Her eyes were warm and intelligent and she seemed very calm under the circumstances.

"Good morning," DI Reece began. "Let's make a start."

DS Lloyd Bright sighed so loudly a few of the other people sitting round the table turned to look at him. DI Reece offered him a cool glare and continued.

"Before I begin," she said. "I'd like to introduce you to Dr Munch. Dr Munch is here in her capacity as one of the leading experts in the field of Phytotoxicology. That is the study of toxins in plants. We all appreciate you coming here today, Dr Munch."

"Thank you," Dr Munch said. "And please call me Fran."

"On the weekend of the May Bank Holiday," DI Reece said. "A reunion party took place in Brightwater Lane, Frisk. The guests booked out numbers 12, 14 and 16 but the party itself was in number 12. Sometime during the night a number of the guests became ill. When the alarm was raised many of them were rushed to hospital and unfortunately Frederick Fisher, Tom Stuart and Rachel Young didn't make it. Tests confirmed all three died because of massive cardiac arrest."

She poured some water into a glass.

"We spoke to the other reunion guests at length," she continued. "And one thing became apparent - nearly every single one of them claims to have no recollection of what happened at that party. My initial suspicion was some kind of benzodiazepine was involved and the tests carried out confirmed this. Somehow nearly all of those guests ingested a drug similar to Rohypnol during the course of the party. Some of the guests remembered a woman who wasn't part of the reunion. Phoebe Green spent a short while at the party and then left. Phoebe's parents have recently moved into the cottage next door to number 12 and Miss Green isn't unknown to us."

DS Bright sat up straighter in his chair and coughed.

"Yes, Lloyd," DI Reece said.

"We haven't been able to tie her to anything, Ma'am," DS Bright said.

"No, we haven't. I am ninety-nine percent certain the source of the drug was a punch bowl most of the guests drank from but unfortunately nobody witnessed Miss Green anywhere near it. We've also spoken to a number of our colleagues in London, and they put a few feelers out, but none of their sources had even heard of Miss Green."

"Dead end, then." It was DS Jeff Hunter.

"A week later on Saturday 11 May," DI Reece carried on, unperturbed. "A group of friends stayed the weekend at number 6 Brightwater Lane. When they returned home all of them became ill. Andrew Knight's condition worsened, and he was rushed to hospital. He died the next morning. Mr Knight had suffered with a heart condition since his late teens. His wife told us something interesting. When they arrived at the cottage on the Friday there was a bowl of strawberries in the kitchen. Of course, the guests assumed they were a welcome gift from the owner of the cottage but when we contacted Mr Needham - that's the owner, he knew nothing about them. All of the guests ate some of the strawberries but it has been confirmed that the dead man ate much more than the others. The doctors who treated him were baffled by his symptoms. Mr Knight suffered from stomach cramps, fever and shortness of breath. I firmly believe those strawberries were poisoned with something. My initial suspicion is they were mixed with the nectar from the common rhododendron."

DC Taylor raised his hand.

"Yes, Robert," DI Reece said.

"I did some more research, Ma'am," the young DC said. "And there have been very few fatalities from people ingesting the rhododendron nectar."

"That's correct," DI Reece agreed. "Dr Munch. Sorry, Fran."

"Thank you, DI Reece," the plant expert said. "DC Taylor is quite right. The toxins found in the rhododendron plant are of the grayanotoxin variety. These are highly oxygenated diterpenoids that are generally there as a deterrent to insects. However, at certain concentrations and in the elderly and very young they can cause very severe problems."

"And people with underlying heart conditions?" DC Taylor said.

"That's right. The first written account of poisoning by rhododendrons can be traced as far back as the 4th Century B.C. in ancient Greece. It's written that King Mithridates of Pontus – one of the first experimentalists with natural poisons, placed the honeycombs of bees that had foraged on the rhododendron along the roadside in advance of the invading army of Pompey the Great. The Roman garrison, believing it to be a gift of the gods feasted on the toxic honey and fell ill. Some of the men died and the rest were easily overcome due to their toxic stupor."

"That's all well and good," DS Hunter said. "Why did Andrew Knight die when the rest of the guests survived?"

"Your colleague has already suggested why," Dr Munch said. "Symptoms of grayanotoxin poisoning range from nausea, salivation and vomiting to more serious complications such as difficulty breathing, bradycardia, hypertension, coma and death."

DC Taylor raised his hand once more.
"It's not necessary to put your hand up every time you want to ask a question, Robert," Di Reece told him.
"Sorry, Ma'am," he said. "There are no conclusive tests that can prove the toxins came from the rhododendrons, are there?"
Dr Munch shook her head. "Unfortunately not. The toxins are broken down very quickly and unless you're able to pinpoint exactly what it is you're looking for, it's very often too late."

"Thank you Fran," DI Reece said. "Moving on – on Sunday 27 May two men attending a stag party at number 12 Brightwater Lane were found dead by some of the other guests. Both men had suffered heart attacks, and both died at roughly the same time. None of the other stag party guests were able to tell us much, but by all accounts both men were fine a couple of hours before they died. Hungover, but reasonably healthy."
"And you believe these men were poisoned too?" Dr Munch asked.
"That's correct. The result of the autopsies was inconclusive – both men died from cardiac arrest, but there was something that jumped out at me. The skin on both men's arms and face was blotchy and inflamed. And their tongues had swollen to almost double the normal size. In the garden next door are two plants that contain toxins that could account for this. Foxgloves and Deadly Nightshades are growing side by side against the fence."
"Interesting," Dr Munch said. "Foxgloves and Belladonna, to give the Deadly Nightshade its less sinister name do contain certain toxins that have the potential to kill. The cardiac glycosides in the Foxglove can cause nausea, vomiting and skin irritation but very rarely anything more serious. Belladonna however, is in a very different toxic league. Its berries contain both atropine and scopolamine and these toxins are so potent that even a miniscule amount can result in paralysis, convulsions and death."

"So, it is possible these men ingested either Foxglove or Deadly Nightshade?" DI Reece asked her.
"The symptoms you described would indicate they were poisoned with a combination of the two," Dr Munch replied. "The glycosides in the Foxglove could have caused the skin irritation and the atropine from the belladonna would account for the swollen tongue and the cardiac arrest. But there is one thing that you need to take into account. A concoction of these two toxic beauties would be extremely bitter, if not unpalatable."
"Are you saying these men would be able to tell they were being poisoned?" DS Bright said.
"Nature is generally kind, detective sergeant. The toxins present in these plants are not there out of malevolence. The bitterness is there to send out warning bells. Much like the brightly-coloured skin of the poison dart frog acts as a deterrent to predators – the offensive taste of these plants tells anything that tries to eat them it really isn't a great idea to do so."

The room fell silent for a moment. DI Reece had invited Dr Munch to the briefing in the hope that she would strengthen her theory about the guests being poisoned by the plants in Rebecca Green's garden but things hadn't gone quite as she'd planned. The evidence against Rebecca was even flimsier now and all Dr Munch had been able to do was confirm it was going to be impossible to prove the sixty-three-year-old woman was responsible for poisoning the guests on Brightwater Lane.

"Let's move on to the next item on the agenda," DI Reece said. "On Saturday 1st June five people were found dead by a woman who'd arrived for a birthday party. Four of these guests had their throats sliced open and the cause of death of the fifth victim is still unknown."
Dr Munch caught DI Reece's eye. "I think that's well outside my realm of expertise. I'll excuse myself there, if I may."
"Of course," DI Reece said. "We appreciate your help."

"I'm sorry I couldn't be of more help. Unfortunately, Phytotoxicology is a relatively new science and it's also an area of medical neglect in both clinical and experimental aspects."

"You've given us something to look at, nevertheless," DI Reece said. "I think this is a good time for all of us to take a short break. We'll reconvene in thirty minutes."

## CHAPTER FIFTY ONE

"What are you doing?" Henry asked.

Rebecca was outside on the patio. The table in front of her was covered in pieces of paper. It was mostly receipts but there were also three sheets of A4 paper and an old calculator on the table.

"Ticking things off lists of course," she said. "It looks like you're off the hook with my birthday present. I've got everything I wanted and I've reached the sky's limit."

"How much?" Henry couldn't help himself.

"I'm just busy with that now."

"I'll stick the kettle on," Henry said. "Although I'll probably need something stronger when you tell me how much you've spent on plants and the like."

He went inside the kitchen and turned on the kettle. He realised he was beaming from ear to ear. He really didn't give a hoot how much Rebecca had spent on her plants and flowers, but he wasn't going to tell her that. No, that would be a very bad idea. He made two cups of tea and took them outside. He placed the cups on the table. "Well? Do I need to go out and get a part-time job?"

"Don't kill me."

The smile on Henry's face grew so wide he had to look away.

"How much?"

"I added up the receipts from the garden centre in Milford and the one in London and it's quite a bit."

"How much?"

"I got a few things that weren't on the list," Rebecca added. "Don't kill me."

"Do I need to sit down?"

"Two hundred in Milford and just over six hundred in Richmond."

Henry nodded but kept quiet. He was expecting it to be a lot more than that.

"Henry," Rebecca urged. "I know it's a lot of money..."
"It's not," Henry interrupted her. "I couldn't care less if you'd spent twice that. Or ten times that much. It's only money."
"Henry Green," Rebecca's tone turned serious. "I'm not sure whether to kiss you or strangle you. And here was me thinking I had to be careful."
"There'll be other trips to the garden centre, love."
"I'm so happy here," Rebecca said. "We haven't had any obnoxious guests for weeks and everything has turned out how we dreamed it would."
"You can't let anything stand in the way of a dream," Henry said. "Wasn't that what the colonel said?"
"I'd better get these receipts filed before they blow away."
"I don't know why you keep all those receipts."
"I can't help it," Rebecca said. "And you never know when you'll need them again."

She picked up the bits of paper, went inside and headed for the living room. She took the hole punch from the drawer and carefully positioned the receipts so there would be two holes. She opened the sideboard and took out the file with the most recent receipts and correspondence in. As she was pulling it out, she spotted something at the back. She almost dropped the file when she realised what she was looking at. On the cover of the book was a strange-looking orange and black frog with blue and grey speckled legs. The title on the front read: *Poisons and Poisonings – Death by Stealth.* Somehow the book Mary had bought her for her birthday had found its way back inside the sideboard.

* * *

"Where were we?"
DI Reece was dog tired. The strong cup of coffee and the twenty minutes of fresh air hadn't helped at all. She was exhausted and the half-hour break had actually made her feel more despondent and confused. Her head felt

thick, and her thoughts were cloudy. All the plant toxin expert had succeeded in doing was confuse things more than they already were and DI Reece and her team were still no closer to the truth.

"The five dead guests at the birthday party two weeks ago," DS Bright reminded her.

"Four." It was DC Taylor. "The fifth man was a stranger."

"That's correct," DI Reece said. "On Saturday 1st June a woman attending a birthday party at number 12 Brightwater Lane found five dead people inside the cottage. Four of them were friends of hers but the man found on top of the couple in the main bedroom was a complete stranger. We've spoken to the other guests who were invited to the birthday party – thirteen in all, and none of these people knew who this man was either. What was he doing there?"

"We've since learned that his prints were on the knife used to kill all four of the guests," DS Bright said. "And traces of blood from the man and woman in the second bedroom were found on his clothing, so it's safe to assume he was responsible for cutting the throats of the guests."

"We still haven't established why," DS Jeff Hunter chipped in. "And why did he wind up dead?"

"We know who he is," DI Reece said. "His driving license was found in a wallet in his jacket. Wayne Slater. Forty-one-years-old. Last known address, 32 Jenkins Street, Peckham East. Mr Slater has quite an impressive track record. Breaking and entering at the age of seventeen – a number of GBH charges and the last one was armed robbery. That one earned him seven years. Not a very pleasant human being."

"What was he doing in Frisk?" DC Taylor asked.

"We don't know that yet," DI Reece admitted. "What we do know is this: he was found dead on top of the bodies of two people we assumed he killed –

he had an envelope with six-hundred pounds in it, and he showed all the signs of poisoning."

"With respect, Ma'am," DS Bright said. "We don't know that for sure."

"The autopsy showed he died from a heart attack. He had inflammation on the skin of his arms and face and his tongue had swollen to twice its normal size. It's exactly the same as the two dead stag party guests."

DS Hunter yawned and folded his arms. "Do you want to know what I think?"

"Go on," DI Reece said.

"I think we're wasting our time with this one. Five people are dead. OK, four of them were probably decent sorts but Wayne Slater wasn't. We've got our murderer – he's not going anywhere, so why waste any more time on it?"

"Because something isn't right about it, Jeff. Something feels terribly wrong. All of the deaths at the HomeFromHome rentals are connected, including the murders of the birthday party guests."

"You're clutching at straws," DS Hunter said. "Seeing connections and patterns that aren't there. Four people got their throats sliced open. They were unlucky – wrong place, wrong time and all that, but to suggest their deaths had something to do with the others is absurd."

DI Reece hated to admit it but she knew DS Hunter was right. It *was* absurd. But right now she didn't have any other theories. She was running out of ideas, and it was only a matter of time before the mysterious deaths of the HomeFromHome guests would be pushed to the back of the queue, destined to remain a mystery forever.

## CHAPTER FIFTY TWO

"There's someone coming up the path," Henry said and opened the curtain wider.

It had been six weeks since the birthday party guests had been slaughtered. It was the middle of July and the school holidays were almost upon them. Colin, Susan and the twins had asked if they could spend a couple of weeks at the cottage and Henry and Rebecca were happy to oblige.

There hadn't been any more trouble at any of the HomeFromHome rentals because all of them had stood empty for weeks. Nobody wanted to come to Frisk after what had happened there. Rebecca had read somewhere that HomeFromHome properties all over the country were feeling the pinch and there was talk of the company's impending closure. The regular sight of the van belonging to Dawson's Cleaning on a Monday morning was now a distant memory and all was quiet on Brightwater Lane.

"Who is it?" Rebecca asked.

"You're not going to believe it," Henry said. "But it's that DI from Bournemouth. She's with a young man this time."

"I wonder what she wants."

"I'm sure we're going to find out."

DI Reece introduced her colleague as DC Taylor. Henry took an instant shine to him. In his forty years as a teacher he'd always been able to spot a bright spark straight away and Robert Taylor definitely fell into that category as far as Henry could see.

He led them into the living room. "Would you like something to drink?"

"No thank you," DI Reece replied for her and DC Taylor. "I just wanted to bring you up to date on the developments in the investigation."

"That's very decent of you."

"Have you found something?" Rebecca said.

"I believe we have. Are you familiar with a man by the name of Wayne Slater?"

"The name doesn't ring a bell."

"What about you, Mr Green?" DC Taylor said.

He looked Henry right in the eye when he said this. Henry wondered if he'd learned this technique off the internet. Did he think an intense stare was a sure-fire way to drag a confession out of someone?

"I can't say I've heard of anyone by that name," he said. "What's he got to do with anything?"

"We'll get to that in a moment," DI Reece said. "Are you sure you don't remember anyone called Wayne Slater?"

"He was forty-two-years-old," DC Taylor added.

"Was?" Henry said. "You mean he no longer *is*, ergo he has ceased to be?"

The young DC blushed. A smile appeared on DI Reece's face.

"Mr Slater is dead," she said. "That's correct."

"I'm sorry to hear it," Henry said.

"You were a teacher, weren't you, Mr Green?" DC Taylor asked.

"There're no flies on this one, are there?" Henry said to DI Keene. "I taught for forty years."

"You taught English at St James's for a few years. Up in Mitcham."

"You've read my CV then?"

"Wayne Slater was a pupil there in the early nineties," DC Taylor said. "That would have been when you were still teaching there, wouldn't it?"

Henry started to laugh. Rebecca gave him a stern look, but Henry wasn't paying her any attention.

"For Pete's sake, lad. You flatter me with your faith in my memory, but you cannot expect me to remember every boy and girl I had the pleasure of teaching over four decades. We're talking thousands and thousands of kids here."

"So, you can't recall Wayne Slater?" DI Reece asked.

"No," Henry said. "No, I can't."

"He got himself into a bit of trouble after school," DC Taylor said. "Had a few run-ins with the law and spent some time inside."

"Then I definitely don't know him. I'm very particular with the people I associate with."

"He always has been," Rebecca confirmed. "It's a bit of a nuisance sometimes."

"OK," DI Reece said in the way detectives always do when a change of direction is on the cards. "You don't remember Wayne Slater. I suppose it's understandable after all these years. Mr Slater was found dead in the cottage next door to yours at the beginning of June."

"That's a shame," Henry said. "Was he one of the birthday guests?"

"He was there uninvited," DC Taylor said.

"We won't go into the details," DI Reece said. "But we found a substantial sum of money inside Mr Slater's pocket. Six-hundred pounds to be precise, in a brown envelope."

"Are you sure you wouldn't like a cup of tea?" Henry asked.

"Thank you, no," DI Reece said. "The thing is, in cases like this we are often gifted certain powers we wouldn't usually have and one of those is the power to look through private bank accounts."

"That is a very special power," Henry agreed.

"And," DC Taylor carried on. "On the Thursday before the brutal murders you made a withdrawal of seven-hundred pounds from a bank in Milford, is that correct?"

"I haven't the foggiest idea." Henry turned to Rebecca. "Do you remember that, love?"

"I can't say I do," she said.

"The bank statement doesn't lie, Mr Green," DC Taylor said.

"Then I must have done," Henry said.

"The strange thing is this," DI Reece said. "Wayne Slater had six-hundred pounds in the envelope in his pocket. Wouldn't you agree that's odd?"

"If you say so. Hold on, I think I do recall taking some money out. Seven-hundred, you say?"

"That's right."

"You're right. I did withdraw that amount. I promised Rebecca she could go to town at the garden centre for her birthday. She couldn't get everything she wanted in Milford so she got the rest in London when we went up for the weekend."

"I have all the receipts," Rebecca added.

"It's an obsession of hers."

"I'll go and get them."

"That won't be necessary," DI Keene said and glanced at DC Taylor.

"Just one more thing," the young DC said.

"You need to practice your Columbo act a bit more, lad," Henry said.

"You claim you don't know Wayne Slater?"

"You say I taught him thirty-odd years ago," Henry said. "I probably wouldn't recognise him if he was sitting here right now. Although that's not likely to happen, is it? Under the circumstances, I mean."

"And you've definitely had no contact with him since school?"

"No."

"How do you explain why your mobile phone number was in his phone records?"

"I would hazard a guess that there is no plausible explanation for it."

DI Reece stood up. "I think that's all for now. We'll be in touch if there are any further developments."

"I'd rather you phoned next time," Henry said. "You've still got my number, I assume?"

"I have. We'll see ourselves out."

"What was that all about?" Rebecca asked when the Bournemouth detectives had left. "All that about the phone records?"

"They were bluffing," Henry assured her. "That young DC has got a lot to learn about pulling off a proper bluff."

Henry knew as soon as DC Taylor mentioned his mobile phone that DC Taylor was bluffing. He'd never been so sure of something in his life. He knew the young detective was bluffing because the phone Henry had called Wayne Slater on was in the drawer in his study. Henry had found it in the bushes where Slater had dropped it, by the fence in the back garden. It was one of Rebecca's old phones – it was pre-paid and even if Bournemouth CID did get their hands on it all they would be able to *ascertain* was the fact that Henry had phoned it on the Friday when they'd arrived back in London.

## CHAPTER FIFTY THREE

Henry looked up from his book. "All's well that ends well."

"I thought you'd given up on that one?" Rebecca said when she read the cover. "I thought Around the World in 80 Plays was terrible."

"It seems different now. Somehow everything seems different now."

It was the first weekend of the school holidays and the summer was in full swing. The air was warm, and the bees were making the most of the feast to be had in the Greens' garden. Colin, Susan and the twins were due to arrive in an hour or so and Henry and Rebecca had never felt happier. All the HomeFromHome properties in Brightwater Lane had been removed from the website and it seemed like the nuisance from the unruly guests was a thing of the past.

"Cup of tea?" Rebecca asked.

"I'd love a cup," Henry said. "Old Greenbow is determined to succeed with the bed trick."

"I have no idea what you're talking about, love."

"Graham Greenbow," Henry elaborated. "The author is going to try his luck with the bed trick where he goes to bed with one woman and leaves it with another. He's going to end up disappointed."

"I give up,' Rebecca said.

A few minutes later she placed a mug of tea in front of Henry. Next to it she placed a book with a photo of a frog on the cover.

Henry looked up at her. "I suppose we ought to talk about this."

"That sounds like a very good idea," Rebecca said. "We've got an hour or so before the kids and grandkids get here. I want to know everything."

Henry told her. He told her he'd found the book when he was looking for an old bank statement. He'd left it alone but a few days later he took it out and read it when everyone else was asleep. A spark of hope had been lit and an idea began to form.

After the first guests died Henry knew exactly what had happened to them and the initial feeling of horror had been replaced with something else. Who were these guests? How dare they come down in their fancy cars and destroy everything they'd dreamed about? It had to stop.

The more Henry read the more he realised the possibilities were endless. A sprinkle of something in a bowl of strawberries and a little bit of something else in a so-called hangover cure and the chances were, he'd hit the jackpot somewhere along the line.

But it wasn't working fast enough. The bodies were piling up but still the guests kept coming and Henry knew he needed something with a bit more meat on the bone. The press was getting bored – they needed something sensational to put out, so Henry gave it to them on a plate. It seemed to do the trick. After the slaughter of the four birthday party guests people stopped coming to Brightwater Lane.

"How long have you known?" Henry asked.

"When the detectives from Bournemouth brought up the bank records, I thought something was odd. But I couldn't quite put my finger on it. I couldn't figure out what the pencil marks in the book meant, either. I told Mary about it and she said she hadn't underlined those passages. And when people kept dying, I actually suspected the colonel's wife."

Henry took a sip of his tea. "That would have been something."

"You acted like I'd lost my mind when that stag party lot were here," Rebecca continued. "I came up with the same idea and you said I was insane. You basically told me never to mention the subject again."

"I'm sorry, love but if it was going to work, I needed to do that."

"How exactly *did* you do it? How on earth did you get away with it?"

"Simple misdirection," Henry said. "That DI was looking in your direction, I could tell, so I gave her a bit of a nudge closer to you. Of course, she wouldn't find anything – you hadn't done anything, but I was left to get on with it in peace."

"How did you even know it would work?" Rebecca clearly hadn't finished with her questions.

"I didn't," Henry admitted. "But the odds were stacked in my favour. The toxins from those plants aren't necessarily lethal to everyone, but you throw an underlying heart problem or an allergy into the mix and combine that with the sheer number of people staying at those damn HomeFromHomes, there's a good chance one of them will drop down dead."

"I can understand the strawberries," Rebecca said. "But how did you poison those stag-do men?"

"A concoction of belladonna and foxglove disguised as a hangover remedy. It tastes like sewage but hangover cures are supposed to taste disgusting – that's the whole point of them. Those lads fell for it hook, line and sinker. You said you only started to smell a rat when Bournemouth CID brought up the bank records? What made you suspicious?"

"I didn't know you'd withdrawn seven-hundred pounds in Milford. It most certainly wasn't to spend at the garden centre. We always use plastic."

"But you didn't say a word."

"Of course not," Rebecca said. "Whatever happens we're in it together."

"Thanks love."

Rebecca closed her eyes and let out a huge sigh. When she opened her eyes again Henry realised she was smiling.

"What?" he said.

"You really are a remarkable man, Henry Green."

"I have my moments."

"What made you think of Wayne Slater?"

"It was actually one of the guests that first weekend who gave me the idea," Henry said and he too smiled. "Nasty bastard on the surface but soft as cotton wool beneath it. That's what Slater was like. All front. But he was thick with it and those types tend to be easily manipulated. I got his details from a bloke that lives not too far from our old place. Got hold of him under the guise of doing an article about the old school and I had him right where I wanted him. I actually liked Slater back then. Good kid gone bad – you know how it goes. I told him what to do and he did it. I left him the money in the cottage, and I knew he would help himself to the wine. It went like clockwork. The dumb bugger even managed to drop the phone I used to organise things with him, but I had that covered. It was one of your old ones and if the police had found it we could have said the intruder purloined it in the break-in. All's well that ends well."

"And now it's all over," Rebecca said. "The kids will be here soon. Can you promise me one thing, though?"

"Of course."

"I think we've got what we wanted. Let's not kill any more guests."

"I don't think there will be any more guests, love," Henry said.

He finished the tea and leaned back in his chair.

"You're probably right though. I don't think it would be a clever idea to kill any more guests."

## CHAPTER FIFTY FOUR

DI Reece paid Rebecca and Henry one last visit. It was late October - soon the clocks would go back, and the nights would become longer. Rebecca and Henry Green didn't care. They were happier than ever in Sea View Cottage and both of them were looking forward to their first winter in Frisk.

The HomeFromHome rentals belonging to Darren Needham and his brother, Keith had stood empty for months now. For Sale signs had been erected soon after the slaughter of the birthday party guests but only one of the cottages had sold in almost four months of them being on the market. Number 11 had been bought by a short man and his wife. Lionel King was different now – he smiled more and made a point to tell everyone who would listen how he'd managed to buy back a property he'd recently sold for almost half the price he'd sold it for. His wife, Diana was doing well. She got out of the cottage from time to time and she seemed a lot healthier than she did when Lionel was forced to sell number 11 Brightwater Lane.

Mary Major still popped in from time to time. The colonel's wife's only gripe was, now that the HomeFromHome guests were a thing of the past she needed to spend more money on batteries for her hearing aids. She wore them almost continually now.

HomeFromHome went bust. The negative publicity from the events in Brightwater Lane proved to be too much – people panicked, and nobody wanted to risk what happened in Frisk happening to them.

Unbeknown to him, Henry Green's actions had merely precipitated the demise of entities like HomeFromHome. In a few months the world as people knew it was about to come to an end. A microscopic force was going to change the way of life of every single human being on the planet and, with countries closing borders and travel restrictions in place, HomeFromHome wouldn't have been able to survive anyway.

But Henry Green wasn't in possession of a crystal ball, so he was blissfully unaware what was brewing right now in China.

Henry didn't need a crystal ball to predict the outcome of DI Catherine Reece's visit. The expression on her face and the fact she had come alone told him everything he needed to know.

When he opened the door to her, he realised she looked even more miserable close up.

"DI Reece," he said. "It's been a while. Is something wrong?"

"Can I come inside?" DI Reece asked.

"Of course. Come in. I'm afraid you've just missed Rebecca. She's popped into the village to pick up a few things."

"That's OK. It's you I came to see."

"You'd better come in then. I'll pop the kettle on."

DI Reece sat down in the living room. "I'll come straight to the point."

"That's always a good start," Henry said.

"I thought you might like to know the case into the deaths of the HomeFromHome guests has been shifted to the side."

"I'm not following you."

"It means top brass no longer see the viability in any further investigation."

"Top brass?" Henry repeated.

"It's out of my hands."

"That's a damn shame. I know how much time and effort you put into it."

"If you think this is over, Mr Green," DI Reece said. "Think again. I may have had orders from above, but I am not letting this lie until I get to the truth."

"I'll make that tea," Henry said.

He left the room and returned soon afterwards with two mugs of tea.

"Do you want to know the truth?" he said.

"That's all I've ever wanted."

"The truth is, Detective Reece," Henry said. "I like you. I always have done, and I can tell you I very rarely say that about anyone. The truth is this: the guests came to Brightwater Lane and made the lives of the people living here a living nightmare. Some of those guests are dead and you're never going to find out exactly what happened to them. That's the truth. I advise you to take what I've just said back to Bournemouth with you and forget about it as soon as you get there."

"I'm afraid I can't do that, Mr Green."

"Then it's going to send you to an early grave. I've said all I'm going to say on the matter. Take it however you like. You haven't touched your tea."

DI Reece looked at the mug on the table then she looked at Henry.

"I'll pass on the tea, thank you."

Henry nodded and smiled at her. "I think that might be a very good idea. Have a safe trip back."

THE END

Printed in Great Britain
by Amazon

79847897R00142